LIGHTHOUSES of Maryland Virginia

HISTORY, MYSTERY, LEGENDS & LORE

Bob Trapani, Jr.

Lighthouses of Maryland and Virginia

History, Mystery, Legends and Lore

First Edition

ISBN 1-890690-17-1

Published by
Myst and Lace Publishers, Inc.
1386 Fair Hill Lane
Elkton, Maryland 21921

Printed in the U.S.A.
in Baltimore, Maryland
by Victor Graphics

Front Cover Photographs by
Bob Trapani, Jr., U.S. Coast Guard and Shirin Pagels

Typography, Layout and Cover Design
by Kathleen Okonowicz

Dedication

All my friends from the Chesapeake Chapter of the United States Lighthouse Society...true keepers of Chesapeake Bay's lighthouse heritage.

—Bob Trapani, Jr.

Acknowledgements

I would like to begin by thanking my dear wife Ann-Marie and our three wonderful children—Nina, Katrina and Dominic, for their constant encouragement in creating this book and for being with me on so many lighthouse excursions that have forged countless family memories together.

Books are team efforts that reveal the many contributions of others—both big and small, but all sincerely appreciated. The book you are holding in your hand is no different. I would like to thank the following lighthouse friends an authors for their kind and invaluable assistance:

Mary Louise Clifford, Sandy Clunies, Betty Collins, Jane Cox, Jeremy D'Entremont, Elinor DeWire, Kathleen Finnegan, Henry Gonzalez, Tim Harrison, Robert & Joyce Holland, Peter A. Jay, Lauren Liebrecht, Paula Liebrecht, Ed Okonowicz, Kathleen Okonowicz, Shirin Pagels, Tony & Alma Pasek, Scott T. Price, Anne Puppa, Mary Ann Ray, Russ Rowlett, Sandra Sableski, Rev. William Simms, Pat Vojtech and Thomas Wade.

For proofreading and suggestions:

Barbara Burgoon, Mike Dixon, Marianna Dyal, Jerry Rhodes, Sue Moncure and Ted Stegura

I also wish to thank four individuals who have had a profound impact on everything I do in the lighthouse community—your friendship is lasting: Mike Baroco, Dennis Dever, Stephen Jones and Harry Spencer, Jr. Finally, I would like to thank the Good Lord—the Divine Author of life itself.

Other books by Bob Trapani, Jr.

Lighthouses of New Jersey and Delaware
History, Mystery, Legends and Lore
Myst and Lace Publishing, Inc., Elkton, Md. 21921
(2005)

Journey Along the Sands:
History of the Indian River Life-Saving Station
Donning Publishing Company, Virginia Beach, Va.
(2002)

Delaware Lighthouses: A Brief History
History Press, Charleston, S.C.
(to be released in 2006)

Table of Contents

Introduction 1

Mystery Shrouds Wreck of Presidential Yacht 4
Assateague Lighthouse, Virginia

Erosion, Storms & Mystery Plague Light Station 12
Back River Lighthouse, Virginia

Storms and Explosion Scar the 'Coffee Pot' 20
Bloody Point Bar Lighthouse, Maryland

Rugged Beacon Steeped in a History of 'Firsts' 28
Cape Henry Lighthouse, Virginia

War Hero Becomes Light's First Keeper 36
Concord Point Lighthouse, Maryland

Keeper and Bride Honeymoon at the Light 44
Great Shoals Lighthouse, Maryland

Rocket Fire Shatters the Night 50
Holland Island Bar Lighthouse, Maryland

Lightkeeper Found Kneeling in Prayer 58
Killock Shoal Lighthouse,Virginia

Railroad Giant 'Swallows' Light Station 62
Lambert's Point Lighthouse, Virginia

Suffering and Mystery Haunt Lighthouse 70
Point Lookout Lighthouse, Maryland

Life in an Iron 'Cheese Box' 82
Seven Foot Knoll Lighthouse, Maryland

Murder Weighs Heavy on Keeper's Mind 90
Sharkfin Shoal Lighthouse, Maryland

Ice Floes Forever Scar Light Station 98
Sharps Island Lighthouse, Maryland

Termites Invade Chesapeake Bay Light 106
Smith Point Lighthouse, Virginia

Collisions & Fire Haunt Offshore Light 110
Thimble Shoal Lighthouse, Virginia

Light Goes Toe to Toe with Mother Nature 120
Thomas Point Shoal Lighthouse, Maryland

United States President Appoints Keeper 130
Turkey Point Lighthouse, Maryland

Prayers to Escape Ice of the Great Freeze 138
Wolf Trap Lighthouse, Virginia

Five Mariners Drown on Doorstep of Safety 146
York Spit Lighthouse, Virginia

Preservation Efforts on the Chesapeake Bay 152
Thomas Point Shoal Light off Annapolis 154
Hooper Strait Light at Chesapeake Bay Maritime Museum 156
Drum Point Light at Calvert Marine Museum 157
Piney Point Light at St. Clement's Island Museum 158

You and I, New Keepers of the Lights 159

Epilogue 160

Selected Bibliography 164

About the Author 166

Bob Trapani, Jr.

Introduction

> *The story of our lighthouses is not about steel and stone and hard lights flashing from lofty towers or bells tolling from low-floating buoys—although they are parts of it, too. It is, first, a heartwarming and inspiring adventure story about the stouthearted men—and women, too—whose courage and devotion to duty made enduring history back in times when the task of keeping the light burning demanded more back-breaking labor and greater exposure to danger than it does today. The long-time keepers of the lights in the now gone Lighthouse Service were men with brine in their blood. To many of them, the brightest and most important light in their world was the one they stood watch over year upon year—often throughout their lives.*
>
> —Hans Christian Adamson
> *Keepers of the Lights*, 1955

Why do we love lighthouses? The reasons are as varied as the lights and their keepers themselves. Over the years, I have marveled at how much the people of the Chesapeake Bay region not only love and cherish their lighthouses, but the Chesapeake Bay as well, and all its wonderful history. Their fierce pride for the waters bordering the states of Virginia and Maryland is only rivaled by the folks in the Great Lakes, who share a similar unshakeable passion for their timeless maritime heritage. At the center of this incredible pride are the lights themselves, shining bright and beckoning us to share in the lure of history and the one-of-a-kind recreation found at the feet of these magnificent sentries of the bay.

Few bodies of water in America possess a richer heritage than the Chesapeake Bay. From the founding of the United States of America, the Chesapeake Bay has played no small part in the building of our nation's greatness—both economically and militarily. From the industrial strength of port cities like Norfolk, Virginia, and Baltimore, Maryland, to the traditional bountiful harvest of crabs and oysters reaped by the Chesapeake watermen, much of the bay's prosperity can be traced directly to the establishment of the lighthouses.

The Chesapeake Bay has the distinction of being the largest inland body of water along the Atlantic Coast of the United States and stretches 169 miles from the mouth at Cape Henry in Virginia to the head of the bay at Maryland's Havre de Grace. Beginning with the completion of Cape Henry Lighthouse on the southern side of the bay's entrance in 1792, a total of 80 light stations were constructed along the Chesapeake Bay and its many tributaries in an effort to safeguard human lives and protect valuable cargo. The first lighthouse built on Maryland shores was Bodkin Point, which was lit in January 1822, and helped guide ships on approach to the nation's all-important Baltimore Harbor.

The establishment of lighthouses—especially in the infancy of our country, was focused first and foremost on marking entrances and critical approaches to ports, thus its inseparable link to America's prosperity. Our nation's shipping interests knew all too well that unless they were successful in ensuring the safety of their precious vessels, cargoes and crews, our nation's sustainability and growth was at perilous risk. Once the Federal government was able to establish a light at some of the more strategic locations, an ongoing effort to better mark our waterways eventually led to "filling in the gaps" along our coastlines where lighthouses and other aids to navigation would be beneficial to shipping.

As much as we are drawn to these stately icons that have served as guardians for all whom have plied the waters of the Chesapeake Bay over the past two centuries, we also cherish the stories and contributions of the lightkeepers themselves. Throughout this time, dedicated men, women—and even children—helped keep the lights burning bright in order to ensure the protection of their fellow man. Countless stories of valor, sacrifice, hardship, mystery, near brushes with death—and sometimes, even death itself—are sprinkled at every turn along the journey of Chesapeake Bay's lighthouse heritage.

Without the keepers and their families, lighthouses would have been powerless to save lives in the days prior to automatic beacons. In a sense, the keeper was the heart and soul of a lighthouse. As a static object, a lighthouse could not feel the joys and pains of life, nor laugh and cry at the ever-changing moments brought about each day. A lighthouse could not save a life or welcome admiring visitors either —but a lightkeeper and his family could do all these things and more.

Lighthouse author Hans Christian Adamson eloquently explained why the lightkeeper was so important, when he noted, "He seeks neither fame nor riches nor creature comforts. He is in truth his brother's keeper." Adamson went on to say, "The keeper and his light has been shunted off the main track by the bulldozer of progress. With the old-time mariner and his three-stick windjammer he has been pushed high and dry on the lonesome shores of yesteryear. But even if he has no place among today's aids to navigation, the old-time keeper and his old-time light do have a place in our history. In his day, he not only did his best with what he had to safeguard the lives of seafarers, but often risked his own life to rescue the victims of the cruel ocean."

Whether seeking to learn about history or endeavoring to preserve the remaining lighthouses on the Chesapeake Bay, there is no separating the keeper and his light. It is my hope that the stories contained within this volume will help in a small way to preserve the incomparable lighthouse heritage of the Chesapeake. Yet despite the fact that many lighthouses have disappeared and the stories of their keepers have faded into time, the beacons still standing here in the 21st century are hardly done making history. In fact, a new generation of keepers has assumed the "watch" over the lights of the Chesapeake Bay.

Therefore, I also hope this book will add more meaning to preservation—and possibly even inspire others to get involved in working to "keep the lights shining," forever more.

Bob Trapani, Jr.
Wells, Maine
Summer 2006

Photo by Bob Trapani, Jr.

Assateague Lighthouse
Virginia

Bob Trapani, Jr.

Mystery Shrouds Wreck of Presidential Yacht

Lighthouses and lightships are every mariner's friend, especially when the weather grows thick and stormy on dark nights. During these anxious times—when the sea becomes like a boiling caldron of froth and chaotic waves raise up on the wings of the wind—a ship captain peers intently over a shrouded seascape to espy that light he trusts to protect him from the dangers of the deep. Despite the powerful guiding beams, murky atmospheres and a mariner's misjudgment occasionally can turn this lifesaving tool into the cause of catastrophe.

An incident such as this occurred on the night of October 10, 1891, when a disobeyed order resulted in a navigational error that sent the *USS Despatch* to a watery grave. The *Despatch*, which served as the yacht for United States President Benjamin Harrison—and Presidents James Garfield, Chester Arthur and Grover Cleveland before him—was an impressive wooden hull steamer 174 feet in length.

The ill-fated presidential yacht left New York—on what would be its final voyage in route to Washington, D.C., by way of the Chesapeake Bay and Potomac River—when the deadly shoals off Assateague Island, Virginia, grasped the prestigious vessel and refused to let go. Up until this point of its voyage, the *Despatch* was sailing along the coast as planned, prompting Lieutenant Cowles, commanding officer of the vessel, to advise deck officers that he was going to turn in for the night and get some sleep.

With the commanding officer resting in his quarters, control of the ship fell to Lieutenant Mulligan. When just off Assateague

Island, Lieutenant Mulligan would make a navigational error that would not only inflict dire consequences to the vessel, but bring eventual shame to his superior, Lieutenant Cowles, in the form of a Naval inquiry. The *Despatch* found itself precariously close to the shoal-ridden waters just off Assateague Island at about 3 a.m. on the morning of October 10th.

Lieutenant Mulligan had changed his superior's "safe night orders" without permission or notification and charted a new course based on what he thought was the guiding light of Winter Quarter Shoal Lightship, located approximately 20 miles out in the Atlantic off the barrier island.

According to an *Associated Press* report in the October 29, 1891, edition of the *Decatur Weekly Republican*, Decatur, Illinois, when asked by Lieutenant Cowles why he altered course, Lieutenant Mulligan reportedly replied, "that he was sure that the red light he saw was that of Winter Quarter, and there was no necessity for keeping the old course."

The newspaper story went on to report that "in response to Lt. Cowles' inquiry as to why he was not called, Lt. Mulligan replied that all seemed well and there had been no apparent necessity for calling him. Lt. Noel, the ship's executive officer, confirmed the fact of the red light being seen, which he was certain was Winter Quarter light, and that he had ordered the change in course." Though the Captain and his crew possessed the most updated charts, what they didn't realize was that the Winter Quarter Shoal Lightship was temporarily removed from service for repairs. Winter Quarter Shoal Lightship would have displayed a red navigational light that was normally distinguished from the nearby Assateague Lighthouse on land, which showed a white light.

So just where did that "red" light come from?

Apparently, the night atmosphere enveloped in a pesky mist made the visible light appear what it was not. Lt. Cowles later informed a Naval inquiry that "it was a good night for seeing lights, but it was a very bad night for seeing the land, being misty. There was but one light visible when he came on deck and that looked red."

Though Lieutenant Mulligan no doubt disobeyed his superior's navigational orders, there seemed to be a consensus from the officers aboard the *Despatch* that indeed the light visible on the horizon was the color red. Observing this and believing it was the beacon of the lightship, Lieutenant Mulligan saw no need to be so far out in the ocean—or so he thought.

The doomed ship thus became ensnared in the hazardous shoals protruding seaward from land some 10 miles. When the ship grounded fast atop the shoals, the crew found itself about three miles north of the end of Assateague Island, and approximately 75 yards offshore. With its crew and all movable items aboard the ship suddenly tossed about the decks of the ship in violent fashion, surprise and panic ensued. An unsigned letter to the *Baltimore Sun* on October 12, 1891, noted that "it was a remarkable sight to see the ship roll, slow and graceful, so near the shore as she lies, listing toward the sea, apparently endeavoring with each surge to reach the shore, but old Neptune holds her in a tight grasp."

The anonymous witness went on to say, "now and then, a crash is heard in the high wind and sea, a davit loosens its hold on shattered planks, (and) moldings, chairs, tables, boxes, etc., spread themselves over the watery surface."

The ship's grinding halt had jolted Lieutenant Cowles from his sleep and prompted him to race topside to assess the devel-

Photo courtesy of Library of Congress

The USS Despatch, *right, served as the presidential yacht until its destruction in 1891, within a mile of Assateague Life Saving Station.*

oping horror. A quick review of the perilous situation revealed the ship was hard fast atop the shoal. To make matters worse, a gale was beginning to rise up on the Atlantic Ocean. Lieutenant Cowles knew all too well the conditions aboard ship would deteriorate rapidly in the face of the growing storm, so with no other choice, he ordered his crew to issue a signal of distress. He later would state, "I never saw worse surf. I knew no power on earth could save her. Water poured into the engine room, and the ship was shattered from stem to stern."

The distress signal was spotted by a surfman from the nearby Assateague Life-Saving Station, which was about one mile south of the shipwreck. Without a moment to lose, the men of the United States Life-Saving Service sprang into action, led by keeper James Tracey. According to the lifesaving and news reports, the crew of the *Despatch*, which numbered 79, was removed from the stricken vessel in less than an hour, with the lifesavers making 10 trips in all back and forth from the site transporting every crewman to safety.

Photo by Bob Trapani, Jr.

The first order Fresnel lens from the Assateague Lighthouse is on display in the Oyster and Maritime Museum in Chincoteague, Va.

The ship's cargo, which was valued at a $135,000—including $30,000 in silverware—was less fortunate, having been completely lost as the vessel broke up in the face of the gale.

The shipwrecked crew was taken to the Assateague Life-Saving Station where they were cared for before leaving for Philadelphia by train. The men left Assateague Island with literally nothing but the clothes on their back, as the *Despatch* was a total loss.

The *Peninsula Enterprise* later recounted the severity of the gale, noting that "the wind has been blowing at about 40 miles per hour, and the tide is the highest for the past two years and has swept our meadows. Many of the sloops and other craft have been blown up into the land to the inconvenience of the owners."

The court of inquiry investigating the wreck of the *Despatch* later concluded that no one was to blame for the shipwreck, thus exonerating Lieutenant Cowles and his officers.

The November 12, 1891, edition of the *Herald Torch & Light* from Hagerstown, Maryland, reported that "the court in its report said that Lieutenant Noel, the executive officer, had evidently mistaken Winter Quarter light for the Assateague Light, which, in the opinion of the court, had gone out temporarily or else was so dim that it could not be seen from the *Despatch*, which passed within four miles of it." The news account went on to note that "the court states that the orders for the night issued by Lieutenant Cowles were safe and careful. The approval of the report by Secretary Tracy removes all allegations against Lieutenant Cowles."

This would seem to have concluded the tragic demise of the *Despatch*, but nearly one month later on December 10, 1891, the beaching of a whale in Ocean City, Maryland, would conjure up the ghost of the shipwreck.

According to reports, a 40-foot sperm whale inadvertently managed to swim over the sand bar at the resort town at high tide, but as the tide ebbed, the massive mammal was trapped and stranded on the beach.

The *Arizona Republican* reported that "all night long his struggles could be heard by the crew of the life-saving station near by. They

Photo by Bob Trapani, Jr.

Assateague Lighthouse on Assateague Island, Va.

sounded like heavy beating of the surf."

With no way of helping the whale return to the water at low tide, all people could do was watch it suffer. The stranded whale eventually died and shortly thereafter, local residents gathered to cut away the blubber. During the process, an amazing discovery was found. According to the *Arizona Republican*, "in cutting opened the monster's stomach there were found a number of empty bottles and a five gallon demijohn corked and sealed, which contained excellent rye whisky. It is supposed that the whale followed in the wake of the United States steamer *Despatch*, which was wrecked more than a month ago, and swallowed the demijohn as it was floated out of the wreck."

Assateague Lighthouse Facts & Figures

1833—The first Assateague Lighthouse was established.

1839—*The Light-Houses, &c. of The United States* notes that the original lighthouse contained 11 lamps outfitted with 14-inch reflectors as its light source.

1850—A letter from The Secretary of the Treasury dated December 20th notes that Assateague Lighthouse contained 11 lamps under the care of keeper Thomas A. Bratten. The report further stated, "Tower needs repairing, as many of the bricks have fallen out of the wall of the tower, and it also wants white-washing; lamps are good, but the old reflectors are quite spotted in consequence of the silver being worn off; oil-butts are also good. I (the inspector) made this light at 11 p.m. off deck at near night, and I pronounced it a very brilliant light. Dwelling is built of brick, and the roof is leaky and wants new shingling; kitchen needs to be lathed and plastered, and the roof also is leaky. The former keeper was dead before this one took charge."

1859—A report from the Light-House Board dated October 25, 1859, noted that "the light-house at Assateague, on the coast of Virginia, has been represented to the board as inefficient. The present state of the structure and illuminating apparatus will not admit of any greater efficiency. The dangerous Black Fish and Winter Quarter shoals extend fourteen miles seaward from

Assateague, and the existing light does not show outside of them. It is respectfully recommended that this light be replaced by a first order light-house, 150 feet high, to be constructed of brick. The cost of such a structure will be $50,000."

1865—A report from the Light-House Board dated October 26th notes that "the increasing dilapidation of the present tower of Assateague has obliged the board to take measures for building a new one, as authorized by act of Congress."

1867—The new (and present) Assateague Lighthouse and keeper's dwelling was completed on October 31, 1867.

1878—*List of Towers, Beacons, Buoys, Stakes and Other Day-Marks* notes the lighthouse is a red brick tower and white dwelling. The optic was listed as a first-order Fresnel lens showing a fixed white light.

1898—The *Annual Report of the Light-House Board* noted "A telephone, having a metallic conduit connection with the telephone line of the Life-Saving Service, was installed in the keeper's dwelling under the appropriation for national defense, and signal-code flags, etc., were furnished."

2004—Ownership of the lighthouse was transferred to the U.S. Fish & Wildlife Service.

To view the gorgeous First Order Fresnel lens from the Assateague Lighthouse, now on display in Chincoteague, visit the:

Oyster & Maritime Museum
7125 Maddox Blvd.
P.O. Box 352
Chincoteague, VA 23336
(757) 336-6117

Photo courtesy of Lighthouse Digest

Back River Lighthouse
Virginia

Bob Trapani, Jr.

Erosion, Storms & Mystery Plague Light Station

The Back River Light Station had an interesting history, dating back to its construction in 1829, but you might say the site was "doomed" from the outset. Stephen Pleasanton, the frugal Fifth Auditor of the U.S. Treasury and man in charge of America's lighthouses from 1820 through 1852, accepted a low bid from lighthouse builder Winslow Lewis to construct the beacon—a man often tagged with the assessment of building inferior light stations.

The lighthouse, which was located at the southern entrance to Virginia's Back River approximately six miles north of Old Point Comfort, would prove to be no exception to the bad reputation that dogged Lewis throughout his career.

Twenty-one years after it was established, the combination of less than quality construction techniques and the eroding soft marsh on which it stood, forced the federal government to act in protection of the site. A letter from the Secretary of the Treasury dated December 28, 1850, cited the fact that contractors enacted various repairs and improvements to the site, including the establishment of a "bridge of joist and plank, with a railing from the dwelling to the lighthouse."

Though the lighthouse was placed on the river's south side amidst a marshy surrounding in a location best suited for navigation, the site was hardly stable. The 1850 letter went on to note that, "the land, which is very low and subject to be overflowed in heavy storms, is washing away."

The vanishing marsh wasn't the only "enemy" that threatened the existence of Back River Lighthouse. Like many light stations in the South during the Civil War, the light station would suffer serious damage at the hands of the Confederate army who did not want the lighthouse to serve as a guide for the Union navy. The vulnerable lighthouse was finally put back in working order by 1863. Fifteen years later the heavy hand of time would exact its toll yet again on the unfortunate beacon.

The *1878 Annual Report of the Light-House Board* pulled no punches when it informed Congress why repairs were once again necessary at the Lewis-built light station. The report stated, "the tower, which was in a very dilapidated condition, a portion in front having been undermined and thrown down by the action of wind and waves, was thoroughly repaired in August and September." In an effort to stave off the ravaging effects of Chesapeake Bay tides and storm surge, the U.S. Lighthouse Service ordered smaller-type stones strategically placed around the beacon's exposed foundation before larger riprap stone weighing three-quarters to one and a half tons were placed atop the protective arrangement.

Though the site still suffered from the erosion despite efforts to ward it off, the light station managed to hold its own over the next 25 years. But a powerful storm, in October 1903, once again placed Back River Lighthouse in a precarious position. The gale's mighty winds pushed seas ashore with such force that the concrete protection wall around the lightkeeper's house was totally destroyed on the bay front. Even the keeper's house itself, which was situated 144 feet behind the light tower, was not out of the reach of the ever-surging seas during the height of the storm.

In fact, by luck there were contracted workers on site endeavoring to build bulkheads to protect the light station from just such conditions. These workers turned out to be heroes of sorts by braving the frightening storm surge to save the light station.

The *1904 Annual Report of the Light-House Board* noted their courageous actions, stating, "the dwelling and the elevated walk leading to the tower narrowly escaped destruction. The repair party, by working day and night for three days, succeeded in saving the dwelling supporting the walkway so that the light might be maintained." The report went on to capture the storm conditions, noting that, "seas dashed to a height of 14 feet against the porch of the dwelling and moved from their places large stones near the tower. The tin roof was partly torn from the dwelling, and the gutters and down spouts were carried away."

Four years later, Back River Lighthouse was back in the news, but this time it would not be because of erosion or storms but death. On July 13, 1907, the steamer *Mobjack* was plying the Chesapeake Bay off Back River when the captain of the vessel decided it would be a good time to conduct a fire drill. Everyone took their positions and began carrying out the drill when tragedy struck. Second Mate W. P. Morgan was struck by a lifeboat as the crew practiced preparations to abandon ship.

The blow threw Morgan, 22 years of age, into the bay. The *Washington Post* noted in the wake of the accident that the Second Mate "was not a strong swimmer and before the steamer could put back and pick him up, Morgan sank." The *Mobjack* searched hard to locate its crewmember but the Norfolk resident was not to be found.

In a strange act of reoccurrence, another sailor would suddenly be thrown into the Chesapeake Bay off Back River Lighthouse two years later on September 5, 1909. Wilbur Miller, a mate for the Seaboard Air Line at Norfolk, got off work with his brother Perry on Sunday afternoon around 2 o'clock and headed for their home aboard the gasoline launch *Virginia Dare*. As the men steered their boat along the bay waters just off York Spit, an unexplained disaster occurred.

Photo courtesy of Lighthouse Digest

An old postcard presents an artistic view of Back River Lighthouse

The *Washington Post* reported that "the bottom of the launch seemed to literally drop out." Shocked by the sudden turn of events, the brothers grabbed their life preservers as the *Virginia Dare* sank below them and tried to swim toward the southerly shore in the face of a strong current. The two men managed to stay together in the water that was thankfully warmed all summer long by the radiant sun before they were eventually separated after dark. Perry made it to the beach below Back River Lighthouse around 2 a.m. on September 6th. Knowing he was near help at the light station, Perry followed the guiding beacon along the shore where he later explained to the lightkeeper about the accident and the fact that his brother was still missing.

The keeper and Perry took to the light station's launch and began their search for Wilbur, later finding him on the beach two miles above the lighthouse. Landing their boat on the shore, the rescuers ran over to the stricken brother and found him totally exhausted and nearly unconscious. In the aftermath of the rescue, the *Washington Post* reported that, "Wilbur Miller, a mate on a Chesapeake Line steamer, is at Back River Lighthouse in a serious condition, as the result of a battle for his life, against the waves and tide."

Photo courtesy of the U.S. Coast Guard

An 1885 photograph of Back River Lighthouse

In May 1931, another person would lose their

life in the shadow of Back River Lighthouse, but this time it would not be accidental drowning—but suspected murder. Dr. Elisha Kane and his wife, Jenny, were apparently visiting the automated light station on a spring day when she reportedly slipped on the rocks at the base of the conical beacon and drowned. Elisha transported Jenny to a local hospital where she was pronounced dead. The purported accident evidently didn't sit well with Jenny's family, which evidently had its doubts about Elisha's story, for the family members had the man arrested for murder.

The murder trial was captured by the media and turned into a high profile event as the news made the papers even on the West Coast. In the U.S. Lighthouse Society's winter 1995 issue of *The Keeper's Log*, writer Charles Elliott states that the family "accused Kane of having an affair with another woman and killing their daughter, Jenny." Elliott goes on to note that Jenny's brother, Walter Graham, "charged he had read a letter in which the supposed paramour, Betty Dahl, urged Kane to 'get rid of Jenny.' "

Kane, who taught romantic literature at the University of Tennessee, stood strongly by his assertion that his wife indeed slipped on the rocks before falling into the water at the light's base. Kane further stated that his wife suffered a heart attack upon her fall, which he maintained was the cause of death. Elisha's father also testified that as a medical doctor, he treated Jenny for a bad heart over a period of thirteen years. One of Jenny's pharmacists and other acquaintances also confirmed the fact that the woman had a heart condition.

The December 10, 1931, edition of the *Athens Messenger* in Ohio carried a story about fishermen who testified at the trial in Hampton, Virginia.

According to the newspaper, "Fishermen who were digging clams in the vicinity of Back River Lighthouse on September 11 added their testimony today regarding the state's contention that Dr. Elisha Kent Kane, University of Tennessee professor, deliberately drowned his wife, Mrs. Jenny Graham Kane." The news report went on to state, "the testimony had to do mainly with screams, which the fishermen said were the outcries of a woman, 'or a man who could scream like a woman.' " In the end, Dr. Kane was acquitted of the murder charges due to a lack of irrefutable evidence.

By this time, the days of Back River Lighthouse itself were numbered. The United States Lighthouse Service, which had automated the light in 1915, finally decommissioned the deteriorating beacon for good in 1936. Over the next 20 years, the granite light tower stood fully exposed to the wrath of storm and tide, its foundation and conical walls slowly crumbling.

The 127 year-old lighthouse finally lost its battle for survival when the remnants of Hurricane Flossy—which had become a non-tropical storm, swept over the Chesapeake Bay region with winds as high as 56 mph and tides 4.5 feet above normal. The storm winds and surge proved too much for the broken beacon, which collapsed into the water on September 27, 1956. Today all that remains of the lighthouse is a pile of rocks about 50 yards out in the bay.

Back River Lighthouse Facts & Figures

1829—A 30-foot lighthouse was established 6.5 miles north-northeastward of Virginia's Old Point Comfort Light at the southern entrance to Back River.

1839—The *Light-Houses, &c. of The United States* listed Back River Lighthouse as containing 10 lamps with 14-inch reflectors as its light source, which showed a fixed white light.

1855—A *Report on the Finances by the Lighthouse Board* dated October 31st notes that "A new revolving machine and reflecting illuminating apparatus, consisting of six 21-inch parabolic reflectors and 6 fountain lamps, were substituted for the old apparatus of 10 lamps and ten 14-inch reflectors, on the 20th March, 1855, which adds very much to the brilliancy and efficiency of this light."

1860—Back River Lighthouse received a Fresnel lens and a new lantern.

1881—The *Annual Report of the Light-House Board* notes that "A new kitchen floor was put in. As an experiment to prevent the drifting of the sands from about the tower, movable screens were made and placed; this was but partially successful; experience in placing them may render them more efficient."

1894—The *Annual Report of the Light-House Board* notes that "The keeper's dwelling, which was too small to accommodate his family, was enlarged by the addition of another story and by other various improvements, so that three habitable rooms were gained. Various repairs were made. The small building used as a kitchen by the working party was left as a summer kitchen for the keeper."

1899—The *Lights and Fog Signals of the United States* describes the Back River Light Station as a "White tower and detached dwelling; lantern black; lower half of dwelling, white; upper half, unpainted shingles; roof, brown."

1914—The *United States Lighthouse Service Light List* notes that Back River Lighthouse showed fixed white light that flashed once every 90 seconds for a 4.5 second duration. The light was listed as shining 33 feet above mean high water and was visible for 11 nautical miles. The fixed light possessed 490 candlepower, while the flash contained 1,800 candlepower. The overall light tower was listed as being 35 feet tall from base to the top of the lantern.

1915—Back River Lighthouse was automated, making it the first lighthouse on the Chesapeake Bay to have its keeper replaced by an automatic light.

1936—The *United States Lighthouse Service Light List* noted that the lighthouse flashed a white light every 10 seconds. The lens was listed as a fourth order with acetylene as the illuminant. The light possessed 750 candlepower.

1936—The U.S. Lighthouse Service decommissioned the beacon.

1956—The remnants of Hurricane Flossy destroyed the deteriorating light tower on September 27, 1956.

Photo by Bob Trapani, Jr.

Bloody Point Bar Lighthouse

Maryland

Bob Trapani, Jr.

Storms and Explosion Scar the 'Coffee Pot'

Some lighthouses possess an architectural flare that inspires boundless admiration, while others were designed from a purely functional standpoint, conjuring up affection rather than exuding breathtaking beauty. Bloody Point Bar Lighthouse falls under the latter description and thus became fondly known to local mariners as simply the "coffee pot."

Bloody Point Bar Lighthouse joined a long and illustrious line of Chesapeake Bay sentinels when it was established 34 miles below Baltimore as the principal guide for watermen seeking the Eastern Bay in 1882.

The beacon, located one mile off the southern tip of Maryland's Kent Island, protected a large number of oystermen, fishing boats and grain-laden schooners seeking the approach to the Miles River, and the towns of Claiborne and St. Michaels during the golden age of lighthouses.

Locals working the water were not the only benefactors from the light's presence. The *1883 United States Lighthouse Service (USLHS) Annual Report* noted that "This light not only marks Bloody Point Bar and the entrance into Eastern Bay, but it is also a useful Chesapeake Bay light, as a straight run can be made from it to Sandy Point buoy, or the reverse, thus avoiding Thomas Point Shoal, should that light be destroyed by ice."

The very next year, the Lighthouse Board would have to be less concerned about the possible destruction of Thomas Point Shoal Light and focus their attention suddenly on the vulnerable Bloody Point Bar Lighthouse. When established, the thought of dealing with the structural integrity of the stout caisson beacon was probably the furthest thing from the minds of the USLHS, but two powerful storms in early 1884 would change that.

The first winter gale hammered Bloody Point Bar Lighthouse on February 29, 1884, with the second following close behind on March 3rd. The one-two punch of the storms, three days apart, inflicted serious consequences on the "coffee pot." Wind-driven waves from the northwest scoured an alarming amount of sand from the caisson foundation, which was established in only seven feet of water. As the violent swells dipped and swirled around the base of the lighthouse and robbed it of stability, the heavy caisson settled and incurred a noticeable tilt.

According to the *1884 USLHS Annual Report*, "The inclination is about 5 feet from the perpendicular at the focal plane." One can imagine the anxiety of the lighthouse keepers who no doubt allowed their minds to roam during idle moments as to whether their home was going to remain upright, especially when subsequent gales would come knocking on their front door. The immediate action of the Lighthouse Board probably brought little comfort to the lightkeepers, but according to the Annual Report, "It was decided to fill in at once about the northwest side of the caisson with riprap stone to prevent further washing of the sand until some means of permanently leveling the structure could be devised."

The riprap stone proved to be a failed endeavor as soundings taken later at the site revealed the discouraging fact that the stone either sunk in the soft mud or was carried away by a strong undertow. In addition, more sand was lost, thus slightly increasing the depth of water in which the lighthouse stood sentinel. To make matters worse, the keepers not only contended with the fear of their lighthouse tilting even further, they also dealt with a serious hazard to their health inside the "coffee pot." According to the *Annual Report*, "The arrangement of flues in the building is faulty, causing much smoke and a large accumulation of pyroligneous acid when fires are used. This will be corrected."

Normal life at an offshore lighthouse—complete with isolation and hardship—was difficult enough for keepers to cope with. But for the men tending the light at Bloody Point Bar Lighthouse in 1883-84, the situation was exasperated by the terrifying tilting episode and the potentially fatal consequences of toxic gas emitting from inside their home as they strove to stay warm and prepare their meals in the dead of winter.

By November 1884, work was underway to straighten the slanting beacon. Contractors dredged the opposite side of the scoured foundation in an attempt to shift the caisson's weight and bring it back into a vertical position. The maneuver was momentarily successful as the structure moved in the proper direction, but workers quickly realized their efforts were futile.

The 1885 *Annual Report* noted that, "The structure could not be kept in a vertical position, although much care was used, but the inclination is less than one-half as great as before."

Resigning themselves to the caisson's permanent affliction, contractors finished their excavation process, and then filled in the diameter of the area with weighty brush mattresses that projected some 30-feet from the edifice. To ensure that the mattresses—designed to prevent further scouring—remained in place, the USLHS had them loaded with vast amounts of small stone. The distribution of weight on the lighthouse was also considered, and during the process, it was deemed advisable to relocate the water-tanks. During May 1885, approximately 760 tons of large stone was dropped around the base of Bloody Point Bar Lighthouse to further ensure as much stability as possible at the exposed site.

Photo by Bob Trapani, Jr.

Following these measures, the USLHS reported to Congress that "It is expected that by this means further scour and consequent settlement will be prevented. When this stone was placed, no apparent change in the inclination of the tower had occurred since November." For the next 75 years, lighthouse life at the "coffee pot" was more normal, and for the most part, uneventful in comparison to its first couple of years. This relative tranquility would vanish in one explosive moment, on April 30, 1960, that would forever alter the future of Bloody Point Bar Lighthouse.

U.S. Coast Guard lightkeepers, Engineman Mark L. Mighall, 19, and Seaman Haywood H. Savage, 20, were on duty at the station, when just after midnight on April 30th chaos suddenly shattered the night solitude.

A fire of unknown origin started on the first floor of the lighthouse in the engine room, and it soon would sweep through the entire structure at alarming speed. The horrified keepers wasted no time running for the station's fire extinguishers in an attempt to somehow contain the flames of the blaze feeding on the wood interior of their home.

Though surrounded by water at their offshore location, the endless supply afforded by the bay was of no use to the Coastguardsmen who were limited to the effectiveness of their hand-held canisters. As the flames began leaping from the adjacent kitchen into a storage room housing volatile drums of fuel and propane gas tanks, the keepers abandoned their final desperate attempts to knock down the expanding inferno.

Engineman Mighall was quoted in The *Baltimore American* as saying, "We would use the extinguishers until the smoke got us, then run outside for air. We did this maybe three or four times until the fire spread into the kitchen and living room." Once the blaze enveloped the storage room, time had run out for the keeper's fire fighting efforts.

The ensuing panic over the flames gnawing away at the tanks housing the explosive fuel left the men with no other choice for survival, so they raced to evacuate the lighthouse before it blew up. Their means of escape was the station's small boat hanging over the side on davits.

The Coastguardsmen thought they were safe from the reaches of the fiery blaze engulfing Bloody Point Bar Lighthouse as their boat was quickly lowered to the waterline, but that's when a frightful frenzy developed. For whatever reason, the lines holding the boat stopped oh so close to the water—about an inch. But without touching the water, the distance might as well been a hundred feet.

"It was just touching the water, but not enough to float the boat free from the davits," says Engineman Mighall. "Neither of us had a knife to cut the block and tackle. We were stuck there—an inch from escape. I prayed—believe me I did." Out of options and distraught as fate hung over their heads, the keeper's perplexing dilemma gave way to elation as an unexplained large wave lifted their boat free, just moments before massive explosions ripped through the Bloody Point Bar Light.

According to the April 30, 1960, edition of the *Salisbury Times,* Seaman Haywood H. Savage of Willis Wharf, Virginia, was treated for minor burns at the Tilghman Island Coast Guard Station, while Engineman Mark L. Mighall of Washington, D.C., was not injured during their attempt to fight the fire at the lighthouse.

The newspaper went on to report that the "State Police said they learned the explosion was set off by a spark that ignited gas or gas fumes in the compressor room of the lighthouse. The structure, with a wood frame over a steel superstructure, was a total loss, police said. The building housed the light and equipment plus living quarters for the two men."

Photo courtesy of the U.S. Coast Guard

This view of the lighthouse shows why it was nicknamed the 'Coffee Pot.'

Valiant Coast Guard attempts to extinguish the fire were unsuccessful and by daybreak, the Bloody Point Bar Lighthouse was a charred cast-iron shell.

The entire wood interior was consumed by the

insatiable appetite of the inferno, thus ending the days of the lighthouse being staffed by Coast Guard keepers.

During the automation process following the devastating fire, the Coast Guard removed all the floors and the brick lining of the circular superstructure, leaving only the cast-iron shell. To reach the optic, a ladder, which extended from the first floor to the lantern room, was installed. Today, Bloody Point Bar Lighthouse remains an active aid to navigation but the beacon is forever scarred by one explosive moment in time that gutted its keepers' home.

Bloody Point Bar Lighthouse Facts & Figures

1882—The lighthouse was lit for the first time on October 1, 1882. The *1883 U.S. Lighthouse Service Annual Report* notes that "A small room for the fog-bell apparatus was put up at the station in February." The report goes on to state, "The structure is similar to that at Sharp's Island, and consists of an iron caisson 30 feet in diameter and 30 feet high, surmounted by an iron tower 37 feet high." The lighthouse's daymark was a brown tower, on a brown cylindrical foundation with a black lantern and was situated in 7 feet of water.

1889—According to the *1899 United States Lighthouse Annual Report,* "The fog bell machine was replaced by one of improved pattern with a different striking arrangement and the necessary change was made in the position of the bell. The copper smoke pipe was renewed, the inflow pipes of water tank were repaired, and the doors and windows throughout the house put in order."

1936—The *United States Lighthouse Service Light List* notes that Bloody Point Lighthouse was equipped with a fourth order Fresnel lens that showed a fixed white light, with 2 red and 1 dark sectors from a focal plane of 56 feet. The white light was visible 12 nautical miles and the red sectors visible for 9 nautical miles, with the illuminating source being incandescent oil vapor. The lighthouse was also outfitted with a fog signal that consisted of a diaphragm air horn that sounded a 3-second blast every 20 seconds (silent for 17 seconds).

1956—The December 31st edition of the *Salisbury Times* newspaper ran a story entitled, "Duck Hunters Have Brush with Disaster." The report came from Stevenson, Maryland, and stated, "Two duck hunters had a brush with disaster over the weekend when their boat sank and marooned them in a duck blind off the southern tip of Kent Island. It was just before dark Saturday when an alert lighthouse keeper at Bloody Point, a mile to the south in the Chesapeake Bay, saw a white flag waving from the duck blind at Kent Point. He called the Coast Guard, which notified the State Police. Two troopers and 10 Kent Island volunteer firemen went to the scene. Two of the firemen rowed out to get the hunters, S. J. Schoolcraft, 41, of Sykesville, and E. D. Plummer, 39, of Chambersburg, Pa. The two hunters were stranded when waves pounded their boat to pieces and it sank. They were suffering slightly from exposure but climbed in their car and left without being treated."

1960—The lighthouse was automated shortly after a devastating fire consumed its interior framework

1997—The *U.S. Coast Pilot* notes that the lighthouse is located "a mile westward of the south end of Kent Island." The publication goes on to say, "A seasonal fog signal is at the light, which is 1 mile due east of a point on the main ship channel, 120.2 miles above the Virginia Capes.

2005—The *United States Coast Guard Light List* notes that Bloody Point Lighthouse shows a flashing white light every 6 seconds, with two red sectors. The white light is visible 9 nautical miles and the red sectors 7 nautical miles.

Photo by Bob Trapani, Jr.

Old Cape Henry Lighthouse

Virginia

Bob Trapani, Jr.

Rugged Beacon Steeped in a History of 'Firsts'

Boston Light Station in Massachusetts is often referred to as the most historic of all American stations, given the fact that the site is widely credited as being the first lighthouse established during Colonial times, in 1716. Indeed, this New England beacon does possess a most enviable resume when it comes to our lighthouse heritage, but there is another rugged beacon that very well might rival the light in Boston—Virginia's Cape Henry.

Being the first lighthouse commissioned by America's newly formed Federal government in 1790, Cape Henry has since become synonymous with our nation's lighthouse heritage, forging indelible moments of history bearing the honor of "first."

Even before the construction of Cape Henry Lighthouse, the ground that would one-day support the stalwart stone sentinel was soaked in history. English settlers landed at the Cape on April 26, 1607, but their leader, Captain Christopher Newport, had second thoughts about the location due to the fact that he "did not like to inhabit upon so open a road." The settlers would eventually choose Jamestown as their permanent settlement, but before they departed the golden beaches along the southern entrance to the Chesapeake Bay, they erected a cross and named the location Cape Henry. It is said, the spot where the settlers erected the cross was that on which old Cape Henry Lighthouse now stands.

Going way back, Virginians have always taken their aids to navigation very seriously.

Just how serious you might ask?

Well, the answer to that question can be found by revisiting an Act passed by the Virginia Colony's Legislature during 1774, in an effort to safeguard mariners from 'mooncussers' or wreckers—and most likely, pirates. The Act read:

> *And whereas, the taking away, removing, sinking, or destroying the buoys to be fixed, may have very fatal results, be it therefore enacted: That if any person, or persons, shall take away or remove without leave or shall willfully sink or destroy any of the said buoys, he or they, on being convicted thereof, shall be adjudged guilty of felony, and shall suffer death without benefit of clergy.*

The first serious discussions to erect a lighthouse on Cape Henry appear to have occurred in 1720, but the Virginia Colony's lack of support from the British government dashed the plans. Subsequent efforts during the ensuing years also failed until 1772, when momentum for a lighthouse was restored and funds were appropriated for the project. Contractors transported over 4,000 tons of stone to the wind-swept site, and the arduous work commenced. Three years later, more funds were necessary but by this point, in 1775, the Revolutionary War overshadowed the light's construction. As the site sat idle, Atlantic winds whipped the exposed beach at Cape Henry to frenzy time and

Photo courtesy of Library of Congress

The new (left) and old Cape Henry lighthouses

again, causing the massive stones to settle beneath daunting depths of innumerable sand granules.

Once the dust of the Revolutionary War had settled, the Colonies each turned over control of existing lighthouses, as well as authority to build new ones, to the newly formed federal government. The first lighthouse project to be appropriated by Congress was the Cape Henry Light Station, which occurred on March 26, 1790. New York architect and stonemason, John McComb, Jr., was awarded this first federal lighthouse construction project. By late October 1792, the 90-foot octagonal sandstone tower was ready to be lit and placed into service.

After 52 years of service, a letter from the Secretary of the Treasury, in 1844, noted that the Cape Henry Lighthouse was starting to show signs of becoming endangered. The lighthouse was built on a tall sand hill overlooking the entrance to Chesapeake Bay; however, according to the report, "By the action of the strong north and northeasterly gales, the wattlings are heaped with sand to their tops, and between them are hollows from 10 to 15 feet deep. They present the phenomenon peculiar to snow storms; as in the sweeping of the gales, if they meet with obstruction, the snow-drifts are formed immediately under its lee by the eddies of the wind." The alarming overview continued, stating, "The light tower, now threatened with destruction, requires an extension of its foundation, from the deep excavation of sand between it, and the first line of wattling, which, in my opinion, can only be permanently and effectively done with stones."

While the swirling winds demonstrated an ability to undermine the light's foundation, a greater dilemma presented itself 28 years later that would eventually usher in an effort to decommission the beacon over serious structural concerns.

The historic sentinel, described as "a frustum of an octagonal pyramid" by the United States Lighthouse Service (USLHS), started exhibiting frightening cracks on its sandstone exterior in 1872. According to the *USLHS Annual Report* for that year, "Of the eight faces of the tower, six of them show on the outside large cracks or openings, extending from the base upward. Four of them are apparently less dangerous than the other two, and alone would not warrant any great apprehensions of danger, but the latter, viz, those on the north and south faces, where the strength of the masonry is lessened by openings for windows, are very bad, extending from the base almost to the top of the brick cylinder, (which is of more recent construction than the outside masonry) and doubtless terminate at the air-space between the outer and inner walls."

The report went on to state, "At present the tower is in an unsafe condition, and there is no way of repairing the damage satisfactorily, and a new one must be built. This old tower has done good service, having been built in 1791, and is now the oldest tower on the coast south of Cape Henlopen; but it has seen its best days, and now, from age and perhaps defective workmanship, it is in danger of being thrown down by some heavy gale. The light is of the second order, and cannot be seen as far at sea as its importance in respect to location demands. It is undoubtedly one of the first lights, in point of importance, on the coast. A new tower should be built at this station without delay, and the light made of the first order."

Less than a decade later, a new Cape Henry Lighthouse was built and first lit on December 14, 1881. The new beacon was another first in the United States, becoming the tallest lighthouse in America to be constructed of prefabricated cast-iron plates bolted together to form its towering height that extended 163 feet. Unlike the original lighthouse with its exterior sandstone daymark, the second Cape Henry Lighthouse displayed alternating white and black vertical cast-iron plates. The new lighthouse was also equipped with a gorgeous first order Fresnel lens, which remains active inside the tower to this day.

Being fully cognizant of the original beacon's immense historic value to the nation as the first lighthouse commissioned by the Federal government, the decision was made to let the original sentinel stand adjacent to the new light rather than dismantling it.

The *1882 Annual Report of the Light-House Board* noted that "The old tower remains as a day-mark, and is also used as a basis for coast survey triangulation." It is plausible that the prevailing thought among USLHS engineers is that the tower would eventually collapse under its own weight as the cracks in the structure's exterior grew larger over time. So rather than undertaking an obvious unpopular move to tear down such a significant and beloved beacon, the USLHS gave the lighthouse a reprieve on life by letting it stand silent sentinel.

In what may very well have been a lighthouse first in America, the Association for the Preservation of Virginia Antiquities (APVA) established a plaque on the historic tower to commemorate the landing of the first white settlers on April 29, 1896. It is unknown whether any other lighthouses in the country at that time were honored with a plaque for their historical significance, but in all likelihood, the establishment of the marker on old Cape Henry Lighthouse was an original undertaking.

According to the booklet *Cape Henry: First Landing, First United States Lighthouse*, by Norma Elizabeth and Bruce Roberts, "For the next three decades the APVA continued to promote interest in the tower and its historic significance. One June 18, 1930, the US Congress deeded the tower and almost two acres of the grounds around it to the Association 'to preserve the light and make it available to the public.' "

Photo by Bob Trapani, Jr.

Old Cape Henry, in the background, and the newer light stand together along the Virginia coast.

This exciting effort may have been the first time in American history where the Federal government transferred a lighthouse to the private sector for preservation and educational purposes—an action that preceded the current National Historic Lighthouse Preservation Act 2000 by 70 years.

Another interesting "first" that occurred at Cape Henry was listed in the *June 1937 Lighthouse Service Bulletin.*

According to the monthly publication from that era, in 1939 the USHLS "established the first distance-finding station in the world as an aid to navigation, using a radio beacon signal synchronized with a sound-in-air fog signal."

In what might be deemed the single most important "first" in U.S. lighthouse history was commemorated at Cape Henry when the federal government officially transferred the civilian United States Lighthouse Service to the military-controlled United States Coast Guard on August 7, 1939. Ironically, the date of August 7th of that year was the 150th anniversary of the civilian lighthouse service, making the ceremony a bittersweet moment for all members of the legendary United States Lighthouse Service. The end of a proud lightkeeping era thus concluded in the long shadow of the nation's first federally built lighthouse.

The fact that the historic Cape Henry Lighthouse remains standing tall in the 21st century would no doubt come as a mystifying surprise to government engineers who predicted its pending doom 134 years ago.

Despite the wrath of hurricanes and winter gales, old Cape Henry endures and is beloved more than ever thanks to the unwavering efforts of the Association for the Preservation of Virginia Antiquities.

Not only is the proud beacon maintained and preserved by APVA, but the nonprofit also enables thousands of visitors each year to scale the steps leading to the old Cape Henry's lantern where an unprecedented view of the seascape and the new lighthouse is afforded. Historic lighthouse preservation is a journey that has no end, and no one has a longer track record of success as "keepers" than APVA.

Old Cape Henry Lighthouse Facts & Figures

1839—The *Light-Houses, &c. of The United States* notes that Cape Henry Lighthouse is 72-feet tall from its base to lantern and its light a focal plane of 120 feet above the water.

1841—A new lantern with plate-glass windows was installed atop the lighthouse and the light source upgraded to eighteen lamps with 21-inch reflectors.

1857—The interior of the tower was lined with brick and its original wooden staircase replaced by a fireproof cast-iron staircase. A second order Fresnel lens was installed to take the place of the inferior lamp and reflector lighting apparatus.

1861—The Confederates darkened the Cape Henry Lighthouse during the Civil War before Union troops recaptured the site and relit the beacon in 1863.

1881—The old Cape Henry Lighthouse was officially decommissioned on December 14, 1881, when the new adjacent, cast-iron tower was first lit.

1930—The United States Federal government transferred ownership of the historic lighthouse to the Association for the Preservation of Virginia Antiquities on June 18, 1930.

To learn more about Cape Henry Lighthouse
and its hours of operation, contact:

APVA Preservation Virginia
204 West Franklin St.
Richmond, VA 23220
(804) 648-1889
www.apva.org

Photo by Bob Trapani, Jr.

Concord Point Lighthouse
Maryland

Bob Trapani, Jr.

War Hero Becomes Light's First Keeper

Fourteen years before the Concord Point Lighthouse was established at the head of the Chesapeake Bay, the man who would go on to become the light's first keeper was leading a courageous defense of his hometown in the War of 1812. Irishman John O'Neill, who held the rank of second lieutenant in local militia, stood up for Havre de Grace and his young country with an indomitable spirit that refused to surrender to the British without a fight.

Havre de Grace, which was originally known as Susquehanna Lower Ferry, reportedly received its name after French General Marquis de la Fayette, fighting for the Colonies in the Revolutionary War, crossed the river in July 1777, and favorably compared the waterfront community to "our own Havre de Grace in France." The name must have been embraced by the locals for the town eventually took on Havre de Grace as its identity.

As with the Revolutionary War, the War of 1812 was not kind to the river town. Though Havre de Grace suffered its share of hardships in the fight for independence like so many other Colonial towns, war's infliction of pain and loss paled in comparison to the damage and suffering the port and its residents were forced to endure.

In *Havre de Grace, an Informal History*, edited by Peter A. Jay, the Havre de Grace resident provides an interesting perspective, writing, "...if the first war with the British created Havre de Grace, the second virtually destroyed it. Congress, at President Madison's request, declared war on June 19, 1812, and almost a year later, on May 3, 1813, a detachment of British troops under Admiral George Cockburn sailed on a raiding expedition up the Bay and put Havre de Grace to the torch."

Apparently the local militia led by Lt. John O'Neill had been following the movements of the British warship *HMS Maidstone* as it maneuvered in and around the head of the Chesapeake Bay, Susquehanna River and Elk River days earlier. For whatever reason, the small battery of cannons on the west side at Havre de Grace decided to "send a message" of sorts as a few rounds were fired from the town at the warship as it returned from the Elk River.

The provocative rounds no doubt enraged Admiral Cockburn, who ordered approximately 400 troops to land on the shores of Havre de Grace and ransack the town for their act of defiance. The British troops wasted little time in destroying the town, which lay in charred ruins about two hours later.

As the troops rowed ashore, Lt. O'Neill and a few other comrades displayed the valor and spunk to briefly counter the raiders by manning the three cannons at the legendary "Potato Battery," which was located behind a breastwork at Concord Point. The battery consisted of a nine-pound and two six-pound cannons but after one of the militiamen was killed by an incoming rocket, the remaining soldiers fled leaving Lt. O'Neill to man the battery himself.

Undaunted, O'Neill continued to fire retaliatory shots at the approaching British troops until the recoil of one of the cannons injured him. After hobbling over to a nearby

Photo by Bob Trapani, Jr.

Interior stairs of historic Concord Point Light in Havre de Grace, Maryland

factory building, O'Neill and four other men regrouped and "made a noble resistance" against the invaders. Their opposition was soon overwhelmed, with O'Neill and a few others taken prisoner by Cockburn's Royal Marines, who transported the men to the *HMS Maidstone*.

Lt. John O'Neill, who was to be shot for his actions, was held aboard the British frigate for three days before Admiral Cockburn decided to set him free. Just why O'Neill was granted his freedom is something of speculation for historians, but legend points to O'Neill's 16-year-old daughter, Matilda, as the lifesaving reason. According to legend, the young woman—at risk of her own personal safety, rowed out to the menacing warship and pleaded with the admiral for her father's life.

Matilda O'Neill lobbied with the admiral that her father, as a commissioned officer of the local militia, should be treated as a prisoner of war and not as a criminal destined to be executed. This news apparently intrigued Admiral Cockburn, who according to legend, allowed Matilda the opportunity to row back ashore to produce her father's commission. O'Neill's brave daughter was able to locate the document and subsequently rowed back to the *Maidstone* to deliver it to the admiral. The book *Havre de Grace, an Informal History* notes that "Cockburn, impressed by her courage, gave her his tortoise-shell snuffbox, which years later the O'Neill family turned over to the Maryland Historical Society."

O'Neill's story doesn't end with his release by the British. By the middle 1820s the pleas for a lighthouse to be placed at Concord Point were being offered up to Congress as maritime activity grew at the head of the

Photo by Bob Trapani, Jr.

The lens of the Concord Point Light

Chesapeake Bay. Treacherous shoals were an extreme hazard to mariners as they transited the Susquehanna Flats near Havre de Grace, and up until the latter 1820s there was no light to protect fishermen and shipping. In addition to the dangerous underwater obstructions, this historic period was one of great prosperity for maritime traffic at the confluence of the Susquehanna River and the upper Chesapeake Bay.

Longtime Friends of Concord Point Lighthouse volunteer Reverend William Simms, in *SOURCE*, touches on this, saying, "At that time, there was a steady flow of goods coming down the river from the resourceful interior of Pennsylvania. Supplies of lumber, farm products and other items were shipped on rafts called 'arks,' and transferred to large sailing ships at Port Deposit for delivery to major ports such as Baltimore." Simms went on to note "about 1,500 arks arrived in Port Deposit the year before the lighthouse was built."

The transportation of goods wasn't the only rising industry around Havre de Grace prior to the Concord Point Lighthouse being built in 1827. The region's growth also spawned a very prosperous fishing industry along the riverbanks of the town.

Photo by Bob Trapani, Jr.

View of the top of the Chesapeake Bay from Concord Point Lighthouse

Buildings large and small were constructed near water's edge to process the lucrative fishing business thriving in Havre de Grace at the time. In fact, the industry encompassed so much of the waterfront the "Lighthouse Service found it very hard to obtain land on which to build the lighthouse," according to Simms.

Eventually the Federal government was able to obtain the necessary land to construct a 39-foot granite beacon along Concord Point's waterfront. The question of who would have the honor of serving as the light's first keeper became an easy choice for the locals of Havre de Grace. Lt. John O'Neill, long recognized as a war hero in the wake of his courageous efforts 14 years earlier against the British, was appointed to the post. O'Neill maintained the position of lightkeeper at Concord Point until his death on January 26, 1838.

In many ways, the history of Concord Point Lighthouse is inseparable from the O'Neill family, for someone bearing this proud name remained as keeper of the light until it was automated in 1920. Following the death of Lt. O'Neill, his son, John, Jr., took over for his father and remained at the post until his death in 1863. Esther O'Neill, widow of the late John, Jr., succeeded her husband and served as keeper until her retirement in 1878, at which time her son, Captain Henry E. O'Neill assumed the duties. Captain Henry stood faithfully by the light for 41 years until his death in 1919.

Photo courtesy of Lighthouse Digest.

This old post card presents an historic view of Concord Point Lighthouse.

The Captain's son, also named Henry, took over for his father but the end was near for Concord Point Lighthouse and the lightkeeping legacy of the O'Neill family as the beacon was automated the next year.

Captain Henry O'Neill no doubt beamed with pride for his family heritage when one of the cannons manned by Lt. John O'Neill during the British invasion of 1813 was salvaged from the muck and mire of the river in 1915 and placed on display near the lighthouse. Today an historical marker pays tribute to the heroics of Lt. O'Neill and is situated just east of the lighthouse.

The book *Havre de Grace, an Informal History* sums up the story of Lt. O'Neill's valor and the history of the Concord Point Lighthouse by noting that "Although it wasn't standing during the famous events that took place on May 3, 1813, through its long association with the O'Neill family it serves as a reminder that peaceful Havre de Grace was once a battleground."

Concord Point Lighthouse Facts & Figures

1827—Havre de Grace Lighthouse was constructed by the renowned Chesapeake lighthouse builder John Donohoo. According to the U.S. Lighthouse Society Chesapeake Chapter web site, "The lantern was originally lit with 9 whale oil lamps with 16-inch tin reflectors."

1854—A sixth order Fresnel lens was installed at the lighthouse.

1914—*United States Lighthouse Service Light List* notes that the Havre de Grace Lighthouse is located "On Concord Point, west side of mouth of Susquehanna River." The publication goes on to record the fact that the lighthouse showed a fixed red light from a focal plane of 39 feet above mean high water, which was visible 9 nautical miles. In addition, the light source was listed as 350 candlepower.

1920—The Havre de Grace Lighthouse keeper was removed and the beacon automated.

1934—*United States Lighthouse Service Light List* notes that the lighthouse showed a fixed green light from a focal plane of 39 feet that could be seen 12 nautical miles. In addition, the publication records the fact that the lighthouse was equipped with a fifth order Fresnel lens powered by electricity, with 570 candlepower. The lighthouse structure was listed as being 43 feet tall from the ground to the top of the lantern.

1961—The *U.S. Coast Pilot* notes that the "Susquehanna River empties into the head of Chesapeake Bay from northwestward 168 miles above the Virginia Capes. The entrance is between Concord Point, marked by a light, and Perry Point, a mile east-northeastward."

1975—The United States Coast Guard decommissioned the lighthouse on November 17, 1975, and later transferred ownership of the tower to the City of Havre de Grace.

1978—The nonprofit Friends of Concord Point Lighthouse was formed to assist with the preservation of the historic site.

1979—Restoration of the lighthouse and keepers dwelling was begun.

According to a Friends of Concord Point Lighthouse handout, entitled *Concord Point Lighthouse, Then and Now,* the lighthouse was "initially located in the shallows and washed for years by the relentless river currents and bay tides, the land around Concord Point Lighthouse became seriously eroded by the mid-1900s. The waterfront foundation was perilously close to disappearing. Hundreds of tons of fill dirt were added to present the shoreline as it appears today."

To learn more about the Concord Point Lighthouse
at Havre de Grace, contact:

Friends of Concord Point Lighthouse
P.O. Box 212
Havre de Grace, MD 21078

Photo courtesy of the U.S. Coast Guard

Great Shoals Lighthouse
Maryland

Bob Trapani, Jr.

Bride and Keeper Honeymoon at the Light

The lighthouse at Great Shoals may no longer be standing, but its memory endures as that of a onetime friend and lifesaver to mariners as well as a comfortable honeymoon suite for newlyweds during one magical week!

Great Shoals Lighthouse, which stood guard at the entrance to the Wicomico River from 1884 to 1966, once guided steamer traffic some 20 miles upriver to Salisbury, Maryland, as well as tired watermen returning from a hard day's work on the Chesapeake Bay at the river's lower end. Yet for all its work as a beacon for safety during its 82-years of service, a blissful week in 1951 might be the most intriguing moment in the light's history.

The October 29, 1972, edition of *The Daily Times* in Maryland contained a story penned by reporter Orlando Wootten revealing a lighthouse secret that apparently was kept private for 21 years. Wootten's fascinating disclosure entitled "Couple Spend Honeymoon on Great Shoals Light," started out with the question, "What can be more romantic than a honeymoon in a lighthouse—especially when it's forbidden?" At this point, even the most casual reader was hooked and eager to learn about this most unusual occurrence.

Wootten set the stage for his article by describing the Great Shoals Lighthouse and its location at the mouth of the Wicomico River for readers unfamiliar with the sentinel, explaining to them that the structure was similar to the one that is now located at a museum in St. Michaels. He went on to paint a picture using words of the light's humanitarian duties, noting, "Its steady beam was a guide to commercial vessels and fishermen returning after dark, groping for the river mouth, and in the bright sunlight the shining structure was a decoration and landmark cherished by all lovers of the river."

Warming the reader's heart with the notion of Great Shoal's noble service and cherished presence, Wootten then began to unfold the irresistible story of a Coast Guard keeper and his new bride embarking on their life of marriage together by spending an enchanted week at Great Shoals Lighthouse—albeit very unofficially! Being a military entity, the United States Coast Guard's strict regulations forbid its lightkeepers from having family on site.

Unlike the days of the civilian U.S. Lighthouse Service where families were many times an integral part of a light station, the Coast Guard staffed many of America's light stations with crews typically consisting of three to four personnel—but certainly not wives, children or other family members.

Electrician's Mate 2nd Class (EM2) Vernon Cooper was one of three Coastguardsmen stationed on Great Shoals Lighthouse in 1951. The *Daily Times* reported the regular duties of the lightkeepers at that time, stating the men "stood watches, kept the light, polished the brass, (and) tended the radio." The account goes on to note, "the lighthouse was, in effect, a real home on the water, complete with a good kitchen, bedrooms, bath, radio room, with the flashing electric light on the top."

Most Coast Guard keepers at offshore lighthouses were young men who looked forward with great anticipation to monthly leave from their water-locked duty in order to spend it with their girlfriend or wife. In the case of EM2 Vernon Cooper, the romance bug took hold of his heart when he met and courted a Somerset County, Maryland, girl by the name of Juanita Bozeman. As Wootten noted in his news account, "the two were smitten with Cupid's dart."

Eventually the couple married in 1951 and was immersed in each other's love—to the point where keeper Cooper was inspired to orchestrate a grand scheme that would permit his new bride and him to be left alone at the lighthouse for seven days. The combination of the couple being on a limited budget and the fact that Great Shoals Lighthouse was the perfect nearby honeymoon getaway that offered plenty of both isolation and beauty, made the offshore cottage on piles too alluring to pass up.

In order for their honeymoon plans at the lighthouse to become reality, EM2 Cooper obviously had to coordinate a great deal of activities under very unofficial circumstances. Wootten keenly noted that "there was a quiet deal with the other two mates, who departed silently in the gloom of night to parts unknown, and the Coopers moved in." The reporter went on to say, "there were no dispatches, absolutely none, to headquarters on the matter, either by radio, postcard, carrier pigeon, or letter in a bottle."

Where the two other lightkeepers spent their week's absence from Great Shoals Lighthouse is unknown. Amazingly, the three men successfully pulled off a daring caper that carried dire consequences for all involved had they been caught—for the sake of friendship and a keeper's willingness to dance with the hand of fate in the name of love.

There were so many things that could have gone wrong with keeper Cooper's honeymoon proposal, but obviously the crew's bold willingness to follow through on it, along with their careful planning, was enough to overcome the odds stacked against them.

The 1972 *Daily Times* article noted that at the time when reporter Orlando Wootten interviewed Mrs. Juanita Cooper, the woman was now a grandmother and looked back on the week at Great Shoals Lighthouse with fondness—though blushing at times as she recounted the adventurous honeymoon getaway. Mrs. Cooper recalled that "It was in July, and there never was more perfect weather. The sun shone all the day and the moon at night."

Photo by Bob Trapani, Jr.

A fifth order Fresnel lens, similar to the one used at Great Shoals Lighthouse

The square seven-room cottage dwelling atop a screw-pile foundation was transformed into a private paradise for Vernon and Juanita. "We had the whole place to ourselves, with not a neighbor for miles, except, for passing boats," said Mrs. Cooper. "I helped Vernon tend and clean the light, did the cooking, went swimming, sun bathed—even took time to fish over the side of the walkway and catch a few perch." Without a crew on hand to assist EM2 Cooper with the duties of a light-keeper, it was crucial that his new bride helped with ensuring the fifth order Fresnel lens shined faithfully each night—not just for navigational sake, but also to avoid unwanted investigation that could spoil their enraptured wonderland.

Following their stolen week of bliss together, the newlyweds settled back into the normal routine as Juanita returned to the couple's home on the mainland and the two "missing" crewmen returned to their post on Great Shoals. After some time, keeper Cooper would be transferred to Cove Point Lighthouse near Solomon's Island and later to Alaska and Chicago before retiring in 1968 at the rank of chief.

Though Juanita experienced some great memories during Vernon's 25 Coast Guard career, nothing erased the memory and charm of Great Shoals Light.

"I really loved that old lighthouse, and just hated to see it torn down," said Mrs. Cooper told reporter Wootten. "We spent a wonderful week there, and no one ever found out. Now that it's gone, the river doesn't seem the same. I never got back to Great Shoals—but I've never forgotten it."

Great Shoals Lighthouse Facts & Figures

1884—The Great Shoals Lighthouse was first lit on August 15.

1914—The *Lighthouse Service Bulletin* noted that "On March 9 C. C. Tyler, keeper, and Gary E. Powell, assistant keeper, of Great Shoals Light Station, Md., brought to the light station a party of four persons from a disabled launch and furnished them food and shelter for the night."

1916—The *Lighthouse Service Bulletin* noted that "On the night if October 30 C. C. Tyler, keeper of Great Shoals Light Station, Md., brought to the light station three persons whose motor boat had become disabled, and furnished them food and shelter for the night."

1942—According to author Pat Vojtech in her 1996 book entitled, *Lighting the Bay: Tales of Chesapeake Lighthouses*, "This light (Great Shoals) and five other beacons on the Potomac River, were blacked out and their fog bells silenced in 1942 as a wartime measure. The lights were later put back into operation."

1966—The Coast Guard dismantled the wooden cottage at Great Shoals Lighthouse and replaced it with a contemporary steel tower atop the original screwpile foundation.

1997—The *U.S. Coast Pilot* noted that "Great Shoals Light, 37 feet above the water, is shown from a white skeleton tower with a black and white diamond-shaped daymark on piles in depths of 4 feet on the north side of the channel, 0.5 mile above the mouth (Wicomico River); a seasonal fog signal is at the light.

Photo courtesy of the U.S. Coast Guard

Holland Island Bar Lighthouse

Maryland

Bob Trapani, Jr.

Rocket Fire Shatters the Night

Lighthouse keepers in the Chesapeake traditionally understood that their occupation was fraught with danger, especially those courageous souls staffing offshore lighthouses in the unpredictable expanse of the bay. From powerful storms and menacing ice floes to unrelenting fears of collision from passing vessels, keepers knew all too well that on any given day, the hand of fate could deliver dire consequences right to their front doorstep.

For all the calamities that could befall a lighthouse and its keepers, being caught in the line of military fire was not a typical concern—that was until one fateful night on February 19, 1957, which forever altered the long-term future of Holland Island Bar Lighthouse.

Though the light station, which was located approximately twelve miles from Maryland's mainland, had a history of mishap, there was no reason for its keepers to suspect that this particular winter night was about to become another peculiar chapter in the annals of their lighthouse. Holland Island Bar's four Coast Guard keepers—Boatswain's Mate 1/C and officer in charge Arnold W. Doyle; Engineman 2/C Donald M. Warner; Engineman 3/C William T. Scott; and Seaman David L. Farrell—were busy carrying out their duties, like any other evening, on that winter night, prior to a moment of terror overtaking their becalm beacon.

It was common knowledge to the Coastguardsmen at Holland Island Bar Light that the United States Navy conducted occasional target practice air missions just to the north of the lighthouse near Bloodsworth Island. In advance of such missions the Navy would take great precaution to alert the maritime community of pending aircraft activities that included air bombing, air strafing, rocket fire and even shore bombardment.

Bombing practice could also occur day or night along the channel of Kedges Straits in the bay, an experience that must have been unnerving for the keepers of Holland Island Bar Lighthouse no matter how much advance notice they received or how many times they witnessed such explosive events. Simply the sound of fighter planes roaring overhead—especially under the cover of darkness, and diving on targets illuminated only by flares—would most certainly rivet anyone's interest on a black seascape that would soon erupt into a detonating din thereafter.

Normally, the light station's crew would have split up their nightly duties so that while two or three men slept, at least one other crewman was up and about watching the light, answering radio checks and busying himself with housekeeping chores. On this particular night, armed with the knowledge that military planes would soon invade their airspace, it is likely that no keeper would sleep through the Navy's *AD-5N Skyraiders* thunderous calling card that reverberated across the bay on their vaporous trails.

True to the Navy's word, three attack bombers soon streaked across the night sky and commenced what they believed was a normal target practice activity designed to fine-tune their aim.

According to the February 20, 1957, edition of the *Salisbury Times*, "the target of the planes was an old sunken ship four miles to the west" of the Holland Island Bar Lighthouse that the Navy dubbed the "Hannibal target." Initially, flying as a threesome, the lead plane soon took off ahead to drop flares in the vicinity of the hulk's watery grave. As the falling beacons burst into a brilliant glow revealing the "prize," the other two Navy bombers zoomed into position and launched their ordnance in the form of five-inch practice rockets whipping frenzy through the air.

Meanwhile, the lightkeepers aboard Holland Island Bar Lighthouse thought they were provided an unobstructed front row seat to the night "fireworks"—not having the slightest inclination that they would soon become center stage in a practice mission gone mad. Without warning, the lighthouse itself fell victim to the rogue rockets, tearing through the structure with blinding speed. In the wake of the stray ordnance, panic and confusion ensued.

The *Lima News* from Ohio reported that "three Navy attack bombers, conducting firing practice after Monday night, apparently overshot their target and scored hits on a Coast Guard lighthouse here." The news account went on to state, "A Coast Guard spokesman said two men stationed at the lighthouse received minor scratches. He said he was told by those on duty that the target in the bay was in line with the lighthouse. Several missiles from the planes apparently went over the target, ricocheted on the water and struck the lighthouse.

The horrified lighthouse keepers scurried about the screw-pile structure as the planes moved off the target to discover that three holes, each about 18 inches in diameter, were blasted through the wooden walls of the cottage. In addition, several tanks containing fuel oil and gasoline on the exterior of the lighthouse were ruptured, but miraculously, the structure was spared the added terror of fire spreading about the light station. Because the fighter planes flew their mission under the cover of darkness, the pilots would not have been able to readily see that their rockets missed the target and skipped along the bay waters

Photo courtesy of the U.S. Coast Guard

before striking the lighthouse. Alerting their superiors of the terrible incident, the Coastguardsmen evacuated the lighthouse. The *Lima News* reported that "the men were taken off the station and were operating from a small boat standing by," not knowing if the structure would be hit again or suddenly burst into flames.

Apparently, the mishap could be partially pinned on the fact that the *AD-5N Skyraiders* were not from the nearby Naval Air Station at Patuxent, Maryland, but from the air station in Atlantic City, New Jersey. Undoubtedly, though the U.S. Navy was embarrassed by the incident, the Coast Guard saw it as an opportunity to convey their unwavering dedication to duty.

The *Salisbury Times* captures this pride, noting that "the Coast Guard said there was some damage but the light used to warn ships of the shallow water remained burning throughout."

This would seem to be the end of the story about how a lighthouse was subjected to unsuspected friendly fire, but three days after the incident, additional details highlighting the disturbing drama on the night of February 19th came to light. The newspaper *Berkshire Eagle* in Pittsfield, Massachusetts, reported to its readers how a rescue mission was initiated immediately by the Navy, as soon as the mishap was reported. The February 23, 1957, edition of the paper ran the headlines, "Navy Flew Dramatic Mission to Aid Shot-up Lighthouse."

The intriguing account whetted the reader's curiosity in the wake of the headline by noting that "the Navy today disclosed the details of a daring helicopter mercy mission and a doctor lowered in the black of night to the roof of a Chesapeake Bay lighthouse accidentally shot up by three Navy planes last Monday, an incident it revealed only yesterday."

The Navy command at the Patuxent Air Station—some 24 miles across the bay from the lighthouse, wasted no time in assembling a crew to fly a helicopter out to the stricken beacon to enact a rescue of its keepers. Initial reports apparently did not indicate the condition of the Coast Guard keepers, conjuring up worst-case scenarios for the Naval command.

Leaving nothing to chance in what at that moment was deemed an urgent rescue mission; the Navy looked to one of their own pioneers—Lt. Commander William C. Casey, a 35-year-old helicopter pilot from Staten Island, New York—to lead the effort. From all accounts, Casey was the best man for the job and a pioneer at flying helicopters under the cover of darkness on instruments alone.

Once appointed for the mission, the *Berkshire Eagle* reports the next sequence of events, stating, "Casey quickly assembled a crew—co-pilot and hoist operator—and picked up a doctor, Lt. Charles E. Cook, 27, of Sioux Falls, S.D., the real hero of the would-be mercy mission. Casey said Cook, 'still in his Navy blues and carrying his little black bag,' had never been up in a helicopter nor had he ever been lowered from one in a sling."

Lt. Commander Casey covered the distance of 24 miles from the Navy air station to the Holland Island Bar Lighthouse out in the Chesapeake Bay in 15 minutes. Upon arriving at the site, the "egg beater" hovered over the screw-pile light from approximately 10 feet while his co-pilot—Lt. (j.g.) J.P. McCullough watched for any threatening obstructions to the helicopter's blades that might be present on the roof of the lighthouse such as radio antennas.

The *Berkshire Eagle* further noted that "the planes, which had accidentally strafed the lighthouse, were not from Patuxent and Casey and his crew had no way of knowing whether, at that very moment, they might be aiming more rockets at the lighthouse and his copter."

The tensest moment of the would-be rescue mission for the doctor onboard occurred when Commander Casey gave the instructions for Lt. Cook to be lowered onto the pitched roof of Holland Island Bar Lighthouse. Yelling over the deafening sound of the copter blades swirling in the black night,

Commander Casey instructed Cook to be careful since his footing atop the structure would be nothing short of precarious. The doctor was also informed that under no circumstances should he let go of the sling that safeguarded his life until he was certain of his surroundings and footing.

Moments later, Lt. Cook was slowly being lowered by 16-year-old Seaman A. Colon, who served as the flight's hoist operator. Once the doctor gave the signal to release the hoist, the helicopter circled the lighthouse until one of the Coastguardsmen helped him inside. According to the *Berkshire Eagle*, "the helicopter stayed in the vicinity until a boat from the mainland arrived at the rocket-blasted tower. Two men had been scratched slightly when the rockets ripped through the building but no others were hurt."

The combination of the friendly fire incident in 1957 and the fact that such a mishap could conceivably occur again—possibly with deadly consequences this time—no doubt, influenced the U.S. Coast Guard to speed up the automation process at Holland Island Bar Lighthouse. Three years later in 1960, the Coast Guard removed its personnel and established automatic navigational equipment at the site.

Holland Island Bar Lighthouse Facts & Figures

1890—The *Annual Report of the Light-House Board* noted that (excerpted) "Work was begun on the next day (September 21, 1889), but because of continued rough and stormy weather little could be done until October...The light was first shown on November 25, 1889, as indicated by the notice issued for mariners. The new structure is hexagonal in plan, with screw-pile foundation, and exhibits a fixed white light of the fourth order. During thick and foggy weather a fog-bell is struck by machinery at intervals of ten seconds."

1931—The March 17, 1931 *Frederick Post*, Md., ran the headlines, "Investigate Death of Lighthouse Man" and reported that "The U.S. Department of Justice today moved to investigate the death of Ullman Owens, keeper of the Holland Bar Lighthouse on Tanger Sound, in the Chesapeake Bay. Owens was found dead yesterday, unclothed and bruised, in the wreckage of his home, after officials were notified the light had not burned since Thursday night. A coroner's jury said death was due to natural causes. Unwilling to accept that verdict, U.S. District Attorney Simon E. Sobedoff sent a Department of Justice official here and orders were given to the sheriff not to permit the body to be buried until the agent had completed his investigation. A local physician who examined the body expressed the opinion Owens had died of a heart attack and believed that while delirious he might have fallen against the pieces of furniture, overturning them and causing the bruises on his body."

1931—The March 20, 1931 *Frederick Post*, Md., ran the headlines, "Probe Death of Light Keeper—Think Holland Bar, Md., Man May Be Rum Runners Victim" and reported that "Possibility that Ullman Owens, keeper of Holland Bar Lighthouse, found dead last Sunday, may have been slain by rum runners was recognized today by a Department of Justice agent here investigating the death. The body of the lighthouse keeper, buried yesterday, was exhumed today and an autopsy performed. Vital organs were removed for examination. People living on the mainland here have told the investigators they believed Owens was killed by rum runners because he talked too much. From his lonely post 12 miles at sea, they said he was nightly in a position to see the boats of a rum fleet claimed to be operating off the shore. They said he knew, perhaps more than any other person, of the operations of the fleet. At the inquest Wednesday here the coroner said death was due to natural causes. The government, however, was unwilling to accept the verdict without an investigation."

1936—The *United States Lighthouse Service Light List* recorded that Holland Island Bar Lighthouse showed a group flashing (two flashes) white light every 10 seconds. The light was listed as shining 42 feet above high water and could be seen 12 nautical miles. The station was equipped with a diaphone air fog signal.

1960—The U.S. Coast Guard dismantled the historic screwpile lighthouse at Holland Island Bar and constructed a modern light tower atop the station's original foundation.

1997—The *Coast Pilot* listed the Holland Island Bar Light as standing 37 feet above the water atop "a white square house with a black and white diamond-shaped daymark on piles in depths of 9 feet on the north side of the bay approach to Kedges Straits." In addition, the publication noted that a seasonal fog signal was maintained at the site, which was listed as being located 72.6 miles above the Virginia Capes.

Photo courtesy of the U.S. Coast Guard

Killock Shoal Lighthouse
Virginia

Bob Trapani, Jr.

Lightkeeper Found Kneeling in Prayer

The guiding light from Killock Shoal Lighthouse was a dependable friend to the watermen of Chincoteague Bay, Virginia, since it was first established in 1886. Not once in the history of the light station had the light's forth order fixed beam failed to shine the way to safety for numerous oyster, clam and fishing fleets that worked the surrounding waters. So you can imagine the surprise of the baymen along the coastal village of Chincoteague on a cold February night in 1912 when the reassuring beam of Killock Shoal Lighthouse did not illuminate the frozen seascape.

The February 14, 1912, edition of the *Iowa City Daily Press* picked up on the mysterious *Associated Press* report, which set the scene for the tragedy at the light station. The news account noted, "At sunset the other day the light from Chincoteague Lighthouse did not shine across the waters on Sinepuxent Bay nor blink the salutation to its sister light at Assateague that guards the treacherous channels and dangerous sandbars of the Atlantic eastward of Chincoteague Island."

All seemed well just a few hours before dusk as the wife of keeper William Taylor bid her husband goodbye as she set off in the light station's boat for the shores of Chincoteague to pick up some much needed supplies. The couple had been prisoner inside the lighthouse for a few weeks due to thick cakes of ice that had encased the structure during a long cold spell.

Once the ice began to break up and run a bit, the hardy woman was forced to set out and battle the floes alone as they could not take the risk of leaving the light station and then not being able to return in time to light the lamp of their fourth order Fresnel lens. The United States Lighthouse Service strictly forbid a keeper from leaving his station abandoned at anytime, let alone at the fleeting moments of daytime when the sun accelerates its descent in the western sky.

As the last glimmers of light were chased from the evening horizon, island residents looked out over the seascape in astonishment at the fact that the Killock Shoal Lighthouse was eerily darkened. Never in the 26-year-long tenure of keeper Taylor had this occurred. Many of the islanders initially surmised that there must be an explanation for the lack of a light but the keeper's wife knew differently. Something inside told her that this situation was not good. Other folks even thought that possibly the menacing ice floes sheered the structure's spindly screw-piles and sent the lighthouse tumbling down, but the idea was quickly banished when someone was able to pick out the structure's shadowy white walls and red roof over the darkening bay.

Mrs. Taylor quickly asked around for a few volunteers who would be willing to accompany her back over the dangerous icebound waters of the bay so she could check up on her husband. She knew all too well that even had the light's apparatus failed, which was possible, that the keeper would have immediately deployed the substitute lamp inside the lens, but this was not the case. The light station remained dark as she readied for her return to the offshore site. The urgency of the situation was captured by the news account that stated, "The light must shine or lives might be lost."

Mrs. Taylor, who was listed as assistant keeper, pushed off from shore with some local men, at which time their strenuous clash with the ice began. The gasoline launch plied its way through the moving floes, and after yeoman's work, arrived at Killock Shoal Lighthouse where they discovered not a single light on in the elevated structure on approach.

The *Iowa City Daily Press* noted that the lack of lighting inside the house "forebode evil." The account went on to state, "as the party drew near and nearer and finally reached the little iron ladder that runs up from the water to the landing platform and were not greeted by the cheerful voice of William Taylor, the keeper, they were convinced that in the few short hours since the departure of the wife something serious had happened."

With great anxiety, Mrs. Taylor rushed up the ladder and inside the lighthouse, with the volunteers by her side. The news account described their findings, stating, "In a few moments their fears were realized, for they found Taylor kneeling at his bedside as if in the act of prayer. He was dead."

In apparent good health, the timing of the keeper's passing proved a shocking mystery. The keeper of the lower lights had gone on to meet the Good Lord on high during an act of reverent prayer—leaving the task of maintaining a light at Killock Shoal to his grief-stricken wife.

Demonstrating the same dedication as her husband, Mrs. Taylor remained on the lighthouse as the men carried the keeper's body across the bay for burial—but not before she brightly illuminated the light's fourth order lens to guide the boarding party safely home across the ice-laden waters. William Taylor was the first keeper appointed to Killock Shoal Lighthouse and remained there with his wife for 26 faithful years, as attested to by the news account, which stated, "Never had the government received any complaint as to its management and the keeper and his wife were esteemed by all who knew them."

Killock Lighthouse Facts & Figures

1888—The lighthouse was built and was referred to as "Killick" Shoal Lighthouse in the early 1900s *Light Lists* and *Coast Pilots.*

1908—The *United States Coast Pilot* describes the lighthouse as a "square, frame dwelling and tower painted white, with lead-colored trimmings and green blinds, surmounted by black lantern (with) red screw-pile foundation."

1908—The Killick Shoal Lighthouse was located in the southeastern end of Chincoteague Bay, where it is entered from Chincoteague Inlet, according to the *1908 Coast Pilot.* The light was the guide at night to the landing at Franklin City, a village with railroad communications on the western shore of Chincoteague Bay, about 5 miles from Chincoteague Island.

2006—Today, only the twisted and deteriorating screwpile frame that once supported the Killock Shoal Lighthouse remains.

Photo courtesy of the U.S. Coast Guard

Lambert's Point Lighthouse
Virginia

Bob Trapani, Jr.

Railroad Giant 'Swallows' Light Station

Many of America's more high profile lighthouses were constructed with the greatest of attention to durability and even a flare for aesthetics architecturally, but Lambert's Point Light Station was not one of them. In fact, the structure, which was located atop a shoal along Virginia's Elizabeth River, may have qualified as one of Chesapeake Bay's "ugly duckling" lighthouses.

The evidence appears to suggest that the lighthouse was established more to satisfy the desire of Norfolk's maritime community for a beacon to warn bustling ship traffic at one of a Virginia's most important ports, than one of seemingly critical navigational importance to the U.S. Lighthouse Service.

The shoal off Lambert's Point, though troublesome, was not overly dangerous to the point where it threatened loss of life or even severe damage to vessels grounding atop the sandy menace. Yet the shoal proved enough of a nuisance to pilots and ship captains, especially during periods of fog, that the lighthouse service agreed to erect a light station at the site—all be it on a low budget.

The old adage, "You get what you pay for," may very well describe the history of Lambert's Point Light Station. and this partly explains why the lighthouse disappeared into the pages of time, only 39 years after being constructed.

The beacon was lit for the first time in May 1872, but even prior to the dwelling being built, the occasional virtue of thriftiness played a huge factor in determining something as important as the structure's screwpile foundation.

According to the *1872 Annual Report of the Light-House Board*, "The original plan of a light-house on six piles was modified, in order to make use of some iron piles that were on hand." When completed, Lambert's Point Light Station was a modest square, wood frame dwelling painted brown and equipped with a fifth order Fresnel lens that showed a red light. The station was also outfitted with a bell, struck by machinery every 10 seconds during times when the river was socked-in by fog.

The lighthouse had hardly weathered its first summer season in 1872 when problems surfaced with the structure's foundation. A few months after being placed into service, Lambert's Point Lighthouse was found to be off-kilter. The dilemma stemmed from the fact that one of the iron pilings on the west side of the dwelling settled some 14 inches into the riverbed. The U.S. Lighthouse Service attributed this situation "on account of an unequal distribution of supplies left at the station, and the soft character of the soil on which the screw-flanges rested."

The reference to supplies left at the station as being the cause of the structure's settling on one side seems to indicate that the contractors who built the lighthouse must have temporarily stored equipment of some nature at the site. Generally, under normal circumstances, supplies required by the lightkeeper typically would not have caused undo strain on the dwelling's pile foundation. In any event, engineers leveled the structure "without difficulty and at little expense," according to the lighthouse service, that undoubtedly was pleased to receive this report.

Rather than replace the settled piling, engineers simply lowered the remaining four piles using a water-jet process, and they further secured the foundation by adding an extra piling on each corner. Following these repairs, the lighthouse service reported to Congress that "the light-house is now firm." Unfortunately, no statement would prove to be further from the truth at the problematic Lambert's Point Light Station.

Nearly every year from 1873 to 1885, the lighthouse required some sort of minor repairs, and in many ways was proving to "nickel and dime" the U.S. Lighthouse Service beyond any valuable return to navigation. Nonetheless, the lighthouse was maintained, and its keepers adequately provided for in typical lighthouse service fashion.

The turning point in the history of Lambert's Point Light

Station—though no one necessarily knew it at the time, occurred in 1885, when the powerful Norfolk & Western Railroad Company made its presence felt in an overbearing way when considering the function of the lighthouse.

The tycoon railway folks established a vast coal wharf that was outfitted with elevated tracks, which extended from the shore right up to the lighthouse. Apparently the U.S. Lighthouse Service and Norfolk & Western Railroad Company did not exactly see "eye to eye" on the new construction.

Undoubtedly, there were concerns on the part of the lighthouse service as to the adverse impact such a massive operation would have on the effectiveness of its lighthouse. In its report to Congress, the U.S. Lighthouse Service bemoaned the situation, noting "the wharf covers a large portion of the light-house site, and the company's works come close up to the light-house on its eastern side."

The encompassing presence of the railway operations were not the only major concern of the lighthouse service as it related to the welfare of Lambert's Point Light Station. It was further noted that the effort to dredge a new channel nearby the lighthouse, which was deemed necessary by port interests in an effort to better

Photo courtesy of the U.S. Coast Guard

Lambert's Point Light Station, and the nearby coal pier

serve deep-draft vessels, had caused the unlucky beacon to settle once again—this time six inches or more on one side.

Whether the condition was truly a concern or exaggerated for political purposes, the U.S. Lighthouse Service informed Congress that the latest encounter suffered by the structure posed a greater risk for fire to overtake the wood frame building. Presumably, their argument was based on the fact that both the structure's heat source (a coal-burning stove) and its light source (which was fueled by oil and flame) could potentially topple and cause a blaze that would most certainly destroy the lighthouse.

In addition to pointing out the Service's anxiety over fire, the report also stated that the dwelling incurred unspecified damages from accidents that one can surmise were inflicted on the lighthouse by the nearby operations of Norfolk & Western Railroad Company. Yet despite the plethora of problems and politics at Lambert's Point Lighthouse, the service conveyed its support—at least publicly, for maintaining the beacon, stating, "owing to the dense fogs and narrow channel, a light-station and fog-bell are needed at the turning point near the present location."

The following year, in 1886, settling of the foundation continued to occur at the lighthouse, prompting the U.S. Lighthouse Service to recommend abandoning Lambert's Point upon the

Photo courtesy of the U.S. Coast Guard

Lambert's Point Light Station, as seen from the river

completion of the new Bush's Bluff Light Station nearby. By 1887, the service was becoming more vocal with its desire to escape the shadow of their indifferent neighbors, informing Congress that the lighthouse itself was "very unsightly, and should be abandoned."

The report went on to place responsibility on the railroad operation for the ongoing problems at the site, noting, "The Norfolk and Western Railroad, which has run its coal-pier entirely up to and around the structure, thereby weakening its foundation, should, however, be required to maintain a light there."

By 1892, the frustration of the U.S. Lighthouse Service over the plight of Lambert's Point reached a boiling point. The *Annual Report* noted once again that the lighthouse was out of level and that the blame could be traced to the railroad's expansion seven years earlier in 1885. Not only did the railway operation surround and dwarf the wooden sentinel, the U.S. Lighthouse Service further lamented the fact that yet "another storage shed has recently been built by the company, which entirely deprives vessels approaching the light-house from up the river of the benefit of its light."

Knowing full well that the maritime community still desired the beacon for navigational purposes, but wanting desperately to remove themselves from a bad situation, the lighthouse service made plans to darken the light permanently. In what may have been a ploy to apply more pressure on Norfolk & Western Railroad Company to assume the costs and maintenance of Lambert's Point Lighthouse, the service noted that "considering the limited extent of its utility it seems inadvisable to incur (any) longer the expense of its maintenance. It has therefore been decided to discontinue this light.

The *1893 Annual Report* read more like a post-mortem as it recounted and justified once again why the decision was made to terminate the duty of Lambert's Point Light Station on December 31, 1892. In responsible fashion for the stewardship of government property, the U.S. Lighthouse Service informed Congress that the illuminating apparatus, fog bell machinery and lightkeeping supplies were removed from the station and placed in storage at Lazaretto Depot for "safe keeping."

At long last, it appeared that the United States Lighthouse Service finally placed the nightmare of Lambert's Point behind it forever, But the hands of fate had other ideas, unbeknownst to the nation's keeper of the lights.

Nearly a decade passed before the "ghost" of Lambert's Point reappeared as a topic of navigational concern in 1901. Though the U.S. Lighthouse Service does not state why it moved to activate the station once more, it is presumed that Norfolk maritime interests garnered enough political support to pressure the service into reestablishing an aid to navigation on site.

According to the *1901 Annual Report,* "the fog-signal was reestablished on the old light-house structure on April 1, 1901, the necessary arrangements to that end having been completed in February. It is a bell struck by machinery a single blow every 3 seconds. The fog-signal had been discontinued since December 31, 1892, when the light was permanently extinguished."

Despite the station's rebirth, the lighthouse structure was in the final stages of its existence.

Years of dredging, which caused the dwelling to constantly settle deeper into the riverbed, ceaseless vibrations from trains working on the wharf overhead and falling objects from the rail operations that inflicted physical wounds on the dwelling below all contributed to the slow demise of Lambert's Point Light

Photo courtesy of the U.S. Coast Guard

The final days of Lambert's Point Light Station shows it tilting to its side, showing the effects of the nearby railroad coal pier.

Station. Add on top of that the unwillingness of the U.S. Lighthouse Service to invest additional monies into what they deemed senseless repairs, it is no wonder that the station and its fog bell went silent in 1911, when the building finally collapsed and "gave up the ghost."

Lambert Point Lighthouse Facts & Figures

1872—A wood frame dwelling surmounted with a lantern was established at Lambert's Point. The lighthouse was equipped with a fifth order lens and fog bell.

1892—The light station was decommissioned on December 31, due to the dwelling being deemed structurally unsafe and the light insignificant to navigation.

1901—The outcry of mariners for an aid to navigation at Lambert Point caused the U.S. Lighthouse Service to reestablish a fog bell at the station, but no light.

1911—The former lighthouse structure at Lambert's Point collapses and is destroyed.

1924—A 14-foot concrete post light with a 250-millimeter lens was established to mark this point and maintained by the City of Norfolk, Virginia

1937—*U.S. Coast Pilot* notes that "Lambert Point, on the eastern side of Elizabeth River, 1 mile southward of Craney Island Lighthouse, is the site of the large coal and other piers of the Norfolk & Western Railroad. The maximum coal loading capacity is 6,000 tons per hour at coal pier No. 4."

Photo courtesy of the U.S. Coast Guard

Point Lookout Lighthouse
Maryland

Bob Trapani, Jr.

9/18/11

Suffering & Mystery Haunt Lighthouse

There is no other Chesapeake Bay lighthouse, and arguably none other in America, which possesses such a connection to grisly suffering and death—all which occurred nearly directly beneath its lifesaving beam—than Point Lookout Lighthouse. In fact, the light station's history is littered with unfavorable circumstances, seemingly bad luck and unexplained mystery.

Built in 1830, the rather drab-looking keeper's dwelling, which is surmounted by a lantern, was originally proposed as a conical tower with a detached house for the beacon's lightkeepers. But the high costs associated with purchasing the land for the establishment of the light station necessitated cutbacks in its design. In the end, it proved less expensive to have lighthouse builder, John Donohoo, integrate the lantern atop the basic dwelling, which at that time, lacked the present second story that eventually was added in the 1880s. The height of Point Lookout's light when completed in 1830 was a mere 24 feet.

Many lighthouses were built in breathtaking locations, and though some of the keepers and their families no doubt enjoyed life at Point Lookout Lighthouse, not everyone possessed the same appreciation for the site

The beacon—which is situated on the north side of the entrance to the Potomac River where it meets the Chesapeake Bay—was once described by a Baltimore district naval officer as "but a bleak, barren sand beach for many acres." The naval officer's keen observation of Point Lookout would later become vivid reality during the Civil War.

In the meantime, the light's first keeper, James Davis, was hardly able to become accustomed to his new post in 1830 when he suddenly passed away two months later on December 3, 1830. His wife Ann took over for her deceased husband and stayed on tending the light at Point Lookout until she too passed away in the line of duty during 1847.

By all accounts, Ann Davis kept an impeccable light station. She even earned the praise of the controversial Stephen Pleasanton, Fifth Auditor of the Treasury, and the man in charge of America's lighthouses from 1820 to 1852. Pleasanton once described her as "one of our best keepers."

The Fifth Auditor indeed held one-time Point Lookout keeper Ann Davis in high esteem, but the same can probably not be said about her successor, William Wood. Though random accidents caused by humans and pets are inherent to life's activities, the penny-pinching Pleasanton must have been furious when he learned that keeper Wood's cat found its way into an open container of precious oil used to illuminate the beacon. Not only did the cat's fall contaminate the light's oil—thus rendering 56-gallons utterly useless—but the feline also broke a crate of 24 glass lamp chimneys. No doubt angry and seeking reimbursement for the damaged government property, the Fifth Auditor withheld keeper Wood's pay for the entire year of 1849 as compensation.

The second female keeper appointed at Point Lookout Lighthouse was Martha Edwards, in 1853. However, Ms. Edwards would only serve two years before passing away in 1855. Pamela Edwards succeeded her mother and remained as keeper of the light for the next 14 years when her tenure ended in 1869. It was during Pamela's service that the serene atmosphere surrounding Point Lookout Lighthouse would be forever banished—replaced by the terrible anguish and gruesome death conjured up by the mid-point of America's Civil War.

In the aftermath of the Battle of Gettysburg, the Union army established a prisoner-of-war camp at Point Lookout. The site, which received its first Confederate soldiers in July 1863, was ideal for Union purposes. The Chesapeake Bay and Potomac River surrounded the sandy spit on three sides, making it difficult, at best, to escape from the prison. Known officially as Camp Hammond, the prisoner-of-war camp was downright hellish for its captives.

According to the *Chesapeake Bay Program's* web site (www.chesapeakebay.net), "The enlisted men were kept in an area known as the "bull pen—one-thousand-foot square surrounded by a 14-foot high fence with guard posts." The account goes on to state, "The men were given only thin tents for shelter, which offered little protection from the sweltering summer hear or bone-chilling cold of the unprotected peninsula. When high tide came, the low-lying 'bull-pen' became prone to flooding, which often resulted in knee-deep mud and swamp-like conditions. To make matters even worse, the flat, sandy soil of the area suffered from poor drainage, and the refuse ditches constantly overflowed into the water supply, making clean drinking water almost impossible to find."

All the while the Union army was escorting Confederate prisoners into this overcrowded and deplorable camp of a reoccurring nightmare, lightkeeper Pamela Edwards was making sure

Photo by Ed Okonowicz

Point Lookout Lighthouse, after undergoing recent restoration efforts of its exterior

that the Point Lookout Lighthouse shined bright each evening. On stifling summer nights when Ms. Edwards would have the dwelling's windows open to permit the movement of refreshing air inside her home, she no doubt must have heard the innumerable cries and groans of dying soldiers filling the nightly air. It makes one wonder if the irony of her situation was realized as she coped with such an unnerving dilemma.

Keeper Edwards' commissioned duties were to ensure that mariners traversing the Chesapeake Bay and seeking the entrance of the Potomac River could observe her guiding beam, which saved untold numbers of sailors from shipwreck and possibly even death at the hands of the sea. Yet, at the same time, Ms. Edwards was sending out her light at Point Lookout, its lifesaving beam was helpless to assist fellow human beings perishing by horrifying numbers in the dark, sinister shadows that were permitted to thrive nearly directly under its golden glow at Camp Hammond.

The prisoner-of-war camp at Point Lookout was only designed to hold approximately 10,000 people, but this number was nearly met in just six months after the facility was established as 9,153 soldiers were confined to this site by December 1863. Rather than alleviating the overcrowding and downright unhealthy conditions, the numbers filed into the camp would grow beyond comprehension—and with it, the magnitude of suffering and death. By June 1865, an estimated 20,000 soldiers were being detained on

Photo by Ed Okonowicz

The entry into the lighthouse cupola is only 14 inches by 20 inches, slightly larger than a standard diner placemat.

Point Lookout. What was once a developing resort of summer fun just prior to the Civil War had now been transformed into a wretched deathtrap for thousands of Confederate soldiers. As if malaria, typhoid fever, chronic diarrhea and scurvy weren't enough, the prisoners also suffered from starvation; often times resorting to eating rats and seagulls just to stay alive.

In all, over 50,000 soldiers and civilians were detained at Point Lookout's prisoner-of-war camp during its 22-month operation, from 1863 to 1865. The sandy spit at Point Lookout would become the final, unceremonious resting-place in mass graves for an estimated 4,000 men, though some argue that the number was grossly deflated and that number could be as high as 14,000. Life would get back to "normal" for the keepers of Point Lookout Lighthouse in the wake of the Civil War; however, the two-year horrendous nightmare that enveloped the location would carry forward in a strange and mysterious manner a century later.

With the last civilian lighthouse keeper at Point Lookout retiring in 1965, the U.S. Coast Guard took advantage of the opportunity to decommission the old beacon as part of the automation process and relocate the light to an offshore spot where it would operate automatically.

The property was sold shortly thereafter to the United States Navy, which had been building a solid presence on the sandy spit since 1951. After 135 years of service, the Point Lookout Lighthouse now stood darkened and silent—lost to another time, it seemed.

The U.S. Navy eventually leased the decommissioned Point Lookout Lighthouse to the State of Maryland parks department. To ensure a physical presence at the site, the parks department established caretakers at the lighthouse in the form of park rangers and employees. At this point, an era filled with sightings of apparitions seems to have emerged from the depths of the bloodstained beaches at the point. Evidently, Point Lookout's dreadful Civil War past is the basis on which people insist that the site is haunted by supposed ghostly characters ranging from Confederate soldiers still roaming the area to a female lightkeeper polishing the lens in an empty lantern.

Ed Okonowicz, a professional storyteller and expert on Delmarva's legend and lore, knows Point Lookout Lighthouse all too well, having visited the site on multiple occasions and interviewing those who swear that they are not alone on this isolated peninsula when the tourists have left for the day. Point Lookout Lighthouse, which is widely considered the most haunted sentinel in all of America, cannot outrun the mystery and legend that looms specter-like over its existence.

In his book, *Phantom in the Bedchamber*, Okonowicz captures firsthand accounts of the unexplained activities swirling around the two-story beacon. The book notes, "According to Donnie Hammett, assistant park manager of Point Lookout State Park, 'Nearly everyone who has lived in the Point Lookout Lighthouse has reported hearing footsteps coming from empty corridors. The mysterious footsteps are so commonplace they are seldom given notice anymore.' Hammett went on to state, 'that those living on one side of the building have said they hear footsteps coming from the living quarters on the opposite side of the building. Also, these sounds always were reported as coming from the second floor,' but 'they have never been explained.' "

Okonowicz quotes parts of a Point Lookout State Park pamphlet that contains testimony by one-time park manager Gerry

Photo by Ed Okonowicz

The names of the Confederate soldiers who died at the prison camp are listed on plaques at the base of the monument.

Sword, stating, "According to the park pamphlet, Mr. Sword had told a lady who was moving into the lighthouse about his experiences while he was a resident in the building. Mr. Sword said he would hear snoring in the kitchen and voices outside the back of the house and in the front yard, too."

Okonowicz goes on to say, "But when he went to check, no one was there. One evening. Mr. Sword said he saw figures of men going through the house, but the sight was never able to be explained."

The woman who listened to Mr. Sword's ominous warning soon became yet another link to the strange occurrences associated with Point Lookout Lighthouse. The unnerving sound of heavy boots strolling along the corridor, a terrible odor emitting from one of the rooms upstairs, sounds of singing, men's voices in the living room and ghostly figures observed in the basement left the female resident to ponder the site's gruesome past during the Civil War.

Was there a connection?

Many people are convinced there is, which has only added to the notion that Point Lookout Lighthouse has earned the reputation as the most haunted lighthouse in America.

Photo by Ed Okonowicz

This monument honoring Confederate soldiers who died at Point Lookout is located near Scotland, Maryland, north of the state park entrance.

Okonowicz summed up his feelings after visiting the

mysterious area for the first time in the late 1990s, noting, "For years readers had been sharing fascinating stories of ghostly activity and unexplained incidents reported at this well-known historical site." Okonowicz went on to state, "Standing at 'the point,' which is, literally, the end of the Earth, surrounded on three sides by the sea, one can immediately understand why the Union decided that Point Lookout would be an excellent site for a prison to hold captured Confederate soldiers. For it was, and apparently still is, impossible for their bodies and spirits to escape from this haunted and hallowed ground."

Point Lookout Lighthouse Facts & Figures

1830—Point Lookout Lighthouse was established and first lit on September 30, 1830. The original dwelling containing a surmounted lantern was much shorter than its present height of 41 feet. When first constructed by lighthouse builder, John Donohoo, the light's focal plane was only 24 feet. Decades later a second story was added to the structure, which subsequently raised the height of the lantern and its light.

1839—The *Light-Houses, &c., of The United States* notes Point Lookout Lighthouse showed a fixed white light illuminated by eleven lamps outfitted with 16-inch reflectors, noting the light could be seen 15 nautical miles.

1872—The U.S. Lighthouse Service constructed a fog bell tower at the site and equipped the tower with a 1,000-pound bell, which was struck by machinery at intervals of 10 seconds. According to the *Annual Report* for this year, it was noted, "this is a very desirable aid to navigation and will be equally valuable to vessels navigating the bay and river." The fog bell was placed into operation for the first time on November 2, 1872.

1883—The *Annual Report of the Light-House Board* notes that "the old roof was removed in May and the dwelling raised one story, for the better accommodation of the keepers. A new tin roof was then put on, and the three enclosed rooms were plastered. New porches were built on the front and back of the dwelling, and various minor repairs were made. The station is now in excellent order."

1883—In addition to enlarging the dwelling, the United States Lighthouse Service also established a new buoy depot adjacent to Point Lookout Light. According to the *Annual Report,* "the distance between the Lazaretto (Baltimore, Md.) and Portsmouth (Virginia) depots was so great, and occasioned so much delay in buoyage work, when the tenders were at intermediate stations distant from either, that it became necessary to establish a depot at Point Lookout, at the mouth of the Potomac River. A wharf, 64 feet by 35 feet, and a buoy-shed, 40 feet by 100 feet, were built there. In the construction of the wharf, 140 piles were driven, and the bridge was extended about 250 feet into the water..." The report went on to further say, "A railway for small cars will be laid from the front of the wharf to and along the front of both (buoy) sheds."

1888—The *United States Lighthouse Service Annual Report* noted that "Since the establishment of the buoy depot at this place complaints have been made that the fog-bell can not be heard, owing to the fact that the coal and buoy sheds, which are higher than the fog-bell tower, intercept the sound. As the bell-frame is partly decayed and must be replaced, the new one will be built in front of and attached to the coal shed." The report went on to state, "In November the water had encroached so far upon the river front of the light-house tract as to cover one end of the foundation of one of the buildings of the depot." The board recommended the construction of a breakwater to remedy this dilemma, which they estimated a cost of $500 for its construction.

1913—The September 1913 *Lighthouse Service Bulletin* cites an action of "Meritorious Service" at Point Lookout Lighthouse. The report notes that "on July 25, Thomas Jacobson, keeper of Point Lookout Light Station, Md., went to the assistance of the occupants of U.S. Navy hydroplane C-1, which was disabled in the water, and towed the boat to shore."

1914—*United States Lighthouse Service Light List* notes that the lighthouse showed a fixed white light of 490 candlepower from a focal plane of 41 feet. The publication also notes the presence of a fog bell, which sounded a single stroke every 10 seconds.

1936—*United States Lighthouse Service Light List* notes that Point Lookout Lighthouse showed a group (two flashes) flashing white light every 20 seconds from a focal plane of 41 feet, with the light visible 12 nautical miles. The light's characteristic consisted of a 2-second flash, eclipsed 2 seconds, and then another 2-second flash followed by an eclipse period of 14 seconds to total its 20-second signature. The light source was a fourth order Fresnel lens illuminated by electricity, with a candlepower of 6,400. The publication notes that the lighthouse was located "on the north side of entrance to (the) Potomac River," and described the beacon as a "lantern on white dwelling." The lighthouse also possessed a diaphragm fog horn that sounded a 3-second blast before falling silent for 17 seconds during its cycle every 20 seconds.

1965—The beacon at Point Lookout was decommissioned.

1997—The *U.S. Coast Pilot* notes that "the shoal (off Point Lookout) that extends about 1 mile southward from the point is marked by Point Lookout Light, 39 feet above the water, shown from a (offshore) skeleton tower with a black and white dia-

Photo by Bob Trapani Jr.

mond-shaped daymark on a pile structure; a seasonal fog signal is at the light.

2006—The *United States Coast Guard Light List* notes that the contemporary Point Lookout Light (offshore skeleton tower) shows a flashing (2) white light every 5 seconds from a focal plane of 39 feet, visible 8 nautical miles. The publication goes on to state, "higher intensity beams towards Smith Point Fairway up Potomac River and northeastward. The structure is described as a "skeleton tower, on piles," with a black and white diamond-shaped dayboard that provides no significant aid to navigation.

To learn more about Point Lookout Lighthouse
and the state park, contact:

Point Lookout State Park
11175 Point Lookout Road
P.O. Box 48
Scotland, MD 20687
(301) 872-5688
www.dnr.state.md.us/publiclands/southern/pointlookout.html

There also is information related to paranormal activity and
ongoing preservation efforts at
www.ptlookoutlighthouse.com

Photo courtesy of Library of Congress

Seven Foot Knoll Lighthouse
Maryland

Bob Trapani, Jr.

Life in an Iron 'Cheese Box'

Unlike the many charming wooden cottages that sat atop the spindly screw-pile light stations throughout the Chesapeake Bay, Seven Foot Knoll was a pioneer effort that yielded one of the bay's most novel architectural designs.

In her book *Lighting the Bay: Tales of the Chesapeake Bay,* author Pat Vojtech commented on the utilitarian sentinel's design, saying, "Sevenfoot Knoll was distinctive not only because it was round, but also because it was the only screw-pile lighthouse built of cast-iron. Baltimore's emergence as a major center of cast-iron building may have influenced the Lighthouse Board's decision to build Sevenfoot Knoll out of cast-iron, instead of wood."

The structure's cylindrical design was neither ornate nor aesthetically creative, prompting some mariners to dub its appearance like that of an oversized iron cheese box. But what was life like for keepers and their families aboard such an isolated circular home surrounded by water—flowing or frozen depending on the time of year? For James T. Bolling, keeper at Seven Foot Knoll from 1872 to 1879, and his family, the realities of everyday living were surprisingly not that much different than their counterparts on the mainland thanks to the family's ingenuity and entrepreneurial spirit.

The notion "home is what you make it" was a lesson learned from a news article that appeared in the October 24, 1877 edition of Pennsylvania's *Chester Times* (reprinted from The *Baltimore Sun*). The story captures a reporter's astounding discovery after accompanying the region's lighthouse inspector on a visit to some of the lights in the bay. Undoubtedly, the reporter had expected a bleak home environment where the family at Seven Foot Knoll was more a "prisoner" of the sea rather than contented dwellers of the circular lighthouse.

The account conveyed that "the visitors climbed a ladder through a trap door and found themselves in the garden, which is an iron balcony running around the cheese-box and filled with flowers growing in pots and boxes, with several children playing in it." The botanical oasis that the reporter observed helped transform the lonely outpost into a cozy abode on iron legs. The gardens were situated along the structure's five-foot-wide exterior gallery surrounding the lighthouse, which was 40-foot in diameter.

The amazement of the visitors did not cease with the gallery's greenery. Once inside, the sight of spacious rooms outfitted with all the comforts of home being occupied by a loving family also proved astonishing. A walk around inside the lighthouse revealed a parlor with a piano and a large sitting room in addition to the expected kitchen area and sleeping quarters. The lighthouse amenities so surprised the reporter that he was inspired to write that the home was "quite as commodious as a French flat in a large city."

The fact that young children lived at the lighthouse with their parents, and seemed contented despite their isolation and lack of neighbor playmates, was a human interest fact not lost on the news reporter. During their stay, the keeper's wife proudly informed the visitors that the children and her were never sick and that their one daughter, Knolie (named after the lighthouse), was even born at Seven Foot Knoll. The young girl had only been to shore once in the first couple years of her young life and as the account noted, "appeared rather shy of the strangers."

The news reporter summarized his unforgettable visit to Seven Foot Knoll Lighthouse and his observation's of the keeper's shy daughter, saying, "three children and two grown people form the child's world, save the broad expanse of waters and the ships that come and go, and the sun and moon and stars overhead. When the ice jams against the piers of the lighthouse in the winter it rocks like a cradle."

The journalist went to on write, "last winter it occupied two men, nearly all the while to watch the stoves and keep them from overturning. Everything was found to be very comfortable and home-like, and the occupants of the singular dwelling were as happy as if they lived on solid land."

Years later (February 28, 1936), The *Baltimore News* published an interview with Knolie Bolling, who was born at the lighthouse on June 23, 1875. The woman recounted her family's stay at Seven Foot Knoll Lighthouse with great fondness. In addition to remembering the large rooms and piano inside the dwelling, she also recalled that her parents had a big bookcase containing a large number of books that contented the family during winter's entrapment aboard the lighthouse. Knolie also remembered having the lighthouse serve a dual role as "school," stating that "Mother had been a school teacher and she taught us, because we had no way to get to and from the shore for school."

As could be expected, some of the most severe storms that played out on Chesapeake Bay during the Bolling's tenure at Seven Foot Knoll made for indelible memories.

Knolie recalls one such storm that came up the bay while her father was caught ashore, forcing her mother to perform heroically as keeper of the light despite having to tend to her young children. Nightfall demanded that the light be lit and kept burning brightly, but the thick weather also meant that the station's fog bell had to sound its audible warning to protect ships in the area. Knolie proudly stated that "my mother tended the light and rang the fog bell all night."

Part of Knolie's childhood memories at Seven Foot Knoll Lighthouse also included the fact that her father kept livestock on a storage platform approximately 8-feet beneath the dwelling. The storage deck, used also as a landing stage for provisions, wood and coal, served as a living quarters for a

Photo courtesy of Library of Congress

A fog bell on the side of the lighthouse

hog pen and chicken yard, thus providing the family with an ample supply of meat and eggs.

Knolie recalled the fact that "several times our 'barnyard' was swept away by storms, but we always managed to rescue the livestock and keep them in our living quarters until father could rebuild their home." Such memories revealed that Keeper Bolling must have been as proficient at serving as a butcher and carpenter as he was a lighthouse keeper.

In fact, author Pat Vojtech stated that "Bolling was one of the more self-sufficient offshore lighthouse keepers in the nineteenth century." As was the case at nearly all water-locked lights, Keeper Bolling had no shortage of fish to supplement his family's diet. The keeper would routinely establish nets and lines from the dwelling's exterior gallery and catch an "abundance of seafood," according to his daughter.

The garden discovered by The *Baltimore Sun* reporter in 1877 contained not only flowers, but vegetables too that the keeper and his family grew in big pots outside on the main deck gallery. Though the ingenious initiative was successful in nature, the effort proved to be very hard work and incapable of supplying the family with an ample supply of much-needed vitamin-laden vegetables. To offset the shortcomings that the family's garden was able to yield, keeper Bolling decided to implement the barter system. He would routinely row to shore—a distance of six miles, and trade his plentiful catch of fish from the bay with farmers for their extra bounty of herbaceous plants.

Though not a duck hunter, this did not prevent Keeper Bolling and his family from enjoying a scrumptious waterfowl dinner now and then. The brilliant beams of light shining forth from a beacon's lantern have traditionally been notorious for "hypnotically" luring seabirds into its glass-pane construction to their death. Seven Foot Knoll Lighthouse was no exception to this phenomenon.

Lighthouse life in the "iron cheese box" was made quite comfortable by the Bollings for facets that they could control, but in the end, apparently the unnerving threat that severe winter ice posed to his family's safety prompted Keeper Bolling to eventually leave Seven Foot Knoll. According to his daughter Knolie, "in spring when the ice broke up, it would pile up against the lighthouse, rocking it and scattering our furniture around. That was what made us change our home finally."

Seven Foot Knoll Lighthouse Facts & Figures

1855—The 42-foot Seven Foot Knoll Lighthouse was constructed in 1855 and lit for the first time in January 1856. The beacon marked the southern approach to the Patapsco River and was situated on the northeast side of the shipping channel to Baltimore. The lighthouse had the distinction of being the first water-locked beacon constructed in Maryland waters and was located 142.1 miles from the capes at the mouth of Chesapeake Bay. The original daymark lighthouse was black with white shutters. The structure was later painted red. When established, the lighthouse was equipped with a fourth order Fresnel lens.

1900—The December 5, 1900, *Nebraska State Journal*, reported that, "A correspondent of the *Philadelphia Press* says that when the late R. E. A. Dorr was on the staff of The *Baltimore American*, news came one day to the city editor that food in the Seven Foot Knoll Lighthouse, out in Chesapeake Bay, was exhausted and that the keeper and his family were starving. Dorr secured a custom house tug and loaded it with provisions. The weather was exceptionally cold, and the tug stuck in the ice a half a mile from the Knoll. Dorr left the boat and started over the ice. When he reached the lighthouse he was warmly greeted, 'Come in the dining room,' said the keeper's wife, after the rescuer had warmed himself. 'Come in and have dinner with us.' Mr. Dorr thought that hunger had made her mad. 'I heard that you needed food,' stammered Mr. Dorr as soon as he could speak. 'Well, come to think of it,' replied the housewife, 'we do. We have plenty of meat and vegetables, flour and that sort but the next time you are coming out this way we'd appreciate it if you'd bring over a few jars of Quince jam,' she added cheerfully. Mr. Dorr took his provisions back to Baltimore but no account of his trip was written."

1913 (January 9th)—*Advocate*, Newark, Ohio stated, "Braved the Dangers of a Storm Swept Sea"...Lighthouse Keeper Sails Six Miles Amid Floating Ice to Secure a Bottle of Father John's Medicine...David W. Collison, assistant keeper of a Maryland lighthouse tells the risks and dangers he experienced in order to secure a supply of Father John's Medicine, as follows: "I am at

Seven Foot Knoll Lighthouse, Patapsco River, Md. I was on the verge of grip. I had previously used Father John's Medicine with good results and needed a supply to give me strength to ward off the attack. Owing to inclement weather, I could not leave the station to go to Baltimore to renew my supply of Father John's Medicine, so I started amid the risks and dangers of drifting ice and sailed six miles to Sparrows Point, where I could secure another bottle of Father John's Medicine. I have every confidence in the medicine and so was willing to undertake the great risk involved." Signed, "David W. Collison"…Disclaimer at the end of the news article… (Father John's Medicine) cures colds and all throat and lung troubles...not a patent medicine and free from poisonous drugs or alcohol...50 years in use.

1933 (September)—*Lighthouse Service Bulletin*..."Keeper Rescue Five from Sunken Tug"...Thomas J. Steinhise, keeper, Seven Foot Knoll Light Station, Chesapeake Bay, Md., has been commended by the Secretary of Commerce for the rescue of five members of the crew of the tug *Point Breeze*, which sank on August 21. This rescue was made in the face of a growing storm.. The tug had sunk almost without warning and its crew had been thrown into the water, scattering in all directions. Despite engine trouble caused by seas breaking over his small boat the keeper reached the men and succeeded in pulling five into his boat before other

Photo by Betty Collins

help arrived. One additional man was found to be dead when he was taken from the water. The rescued men were taken to the lighthouse, suffering from exhaustion and exposure to the high wind, and were temporarily cared for.

1936—*Lighthouse Service Bulletin*, "Lighthouse Keeper Awarded Silver Life-Saving Medal"...Thomas J. Steinhise, keeper of Seven Foot Knoll Light Station, Md., has recently been awarded a silver life-saving medal by the Treasury Department for his service in rescuing five men from drowning when the tug *Point Breeze* sank during a storm on August 21, 1933. The keeper rescued a sixth man who was found to be dead when taken from the water. This rescue was made with difficulty because of engine trouble caused by seas breaking over the keeper's small boat. An item regarding this matter appeared in the *Lighthouse Service Bulletin* for September 1933.

1988—The lighthouse was finally moved to the Inner Harbor in Baltimore. According to the Baltimore Maritime Museum web site, "from 1856 until 1919, keepers at Seven Foot Knoll lived in the lighthouse along with their families. Between 1919 and 1948 keepers worked in pairs, with each receiving 8 days of shore leave per month." The account goes on to state that "the lighthouse was automated in 1949 and the Coast Guard maintained the light, but unfortunately the structure fell victim to its age and the elements. By the late 1960s, plans were underway to retire the light and replace it with a new navigation marker."

1989—The U.S. Coast Guard donated the lighthouse to the City of Baltimore, where it stands in the Inner Harbor (see page 88).

1997—Seven Foot Knoll Lighthouse became part of the Baltimore Maritime Museum and is maintained by the Living Classrooms Foundation. The lighthouse is open, along with the lightship *Chesapeake*. (There is a museum admission fee.)

To learn more about the Living Classrooms Foundation
and the Baltimore Maritime Museum, visit:
http://www.livingclassrooms.org/
http://www.baltomaritimemuseum.org/lh/sevenfootknoll.html

Photo courtesy of the U.S. Coast Guard

Sharkfin Shoal Lighthouse

Maryland

Bob Trapani, Jr.

Murder Weighs Heavy on Light Keeper's Mind

The inherent isolation and long periods of idleness that were inescapable at offshore lighthouses may have suited some keepers just fine, but for a young Coastguardsman in 1948, duty at Sharkfin Shoal Light Station was more like solitary confinement. The lonesome lighthouse, which stood in Fishing Bay off Maryland's Eastern Shore, allowed for the keeper's personal troubles to gnaw away at his mind and turn peaceful solitude into a perpetual nightmare.

Though a seaman in rank with the U.S. Coast Guard, the young keeper, 22 years of age, was no rookie to military service. Prior to enlisting in the Coast Guard during 1946, he was a U.S. Navy combat veteran of World War II. After being discharged from the Navy, the fellow was unable to find steady work, with only a part-time job paying 56 cents per hour to support his young wife and baby. He thus joined the Coast Guard and was stationed in Baltimore, Maryland, before being reassigned to the offshore screwpile Sharkfin Shoal Lighthouse.

Life was apparently not easy for the 22-year-old husband and father, who married in 1946, with the couple's first child being born in March 1947. The combination of mounting debts, his wife's unspecified medical condition and a job that prevented him from being home very much, forced his wife to move in with her parents. Yet knowing that his wife was being cared for seemed little comfort to the keeper, as the need for more money continued to plague the young man and his family.

In the spring of 1948, the troubling financial situation got the best of him. On leave from Sharkfin Shoal Lighthouse, the young keeper resorted to armed robbery while in Baltimore in an attempt to obtain some quick cash. The keeper hailed a cab once on shore and told the cab driver to take him to the Coast Guard station. Upon arrival, the keeper clubbed the cabbie over the head. The cab driver flung open his car door and tried to leap from the vehicle, at which time the lightkeeper shot the driver in the shoulder. The cabbie's wound was not fatal, and it is not clear from news accounts as to whether the keeper obtained any money from his victim, but after firing the shot, the Coastguardsman fled the scene.

The apparent failed robbery attempt did little to deter the desperate young man, when six days later he repeated the tactic of hailing a cab with the intent to obtain money by force. This time the keeper's reckless actions would lead to tragic consequences for the cab driver, who was working the night shift.

According Maryland's *Frederick News*, the cabbie "was a 25-year-old veteran, who had worked in an airplane factory and had been driving a cab for about two weeks as a temporary thing."

Rather than having the cab deliver him to the Coast Guard station like the previous robbery attempt, the keeper directed the unsuspecting driver to an unspecified Baltimore address. Once the cab pulled into a dark back alley, the passenger pulled a gun and uttered, "This is a hold-up." The driver instantly swung around in his seat at which time the startled lighthouse keeper shot the cab driver at point blank range. A bullet wound to the heart proved to be fatal.

Wasting no time in robbing the fallen cab driver, the shooter fled the scene before police could arrive. The *Frederick News* noted that "A couple just going to bed at their home in a northwest Baltimore housing development heard a car drive up in their alley. They heard a shot. From their bedroom window they saw a cab, with a man running away from it. [The cab driver's] empty wallet was found several blocks away."

In both robbery attempts, no one got more than a dim glimpse at the perpetrator, and police were left with very little in the way of clues to go on. Inconclusive descriptions and the bullets removed from the first victim's shoulder and second cabbie's heart were about the only solid clues police gleaned in an effort to solve the crime and bring the individual responsible for the shootings to justice.

Meanwhile, the keeper returned to the Coast Guard station in Baltimore, and when his leave expired resumed his duty at Sharkfin Shoal Lighthouse. The solitude afforded by the light station's remote location in Chesapeake Bay equated to ceaseless mental torment, for no matter how far he was from the scene of the crime, the keeper could not escape the mental anguish that haunted him while he tended the light.

The young keeper's rash actions were unbeknownst to his fellow Coastguardsmen all the while, as they worked together for the next months ensuring the fixed white light and fog bell at Sharkfin Shoal continued to warn and protect mariners on the Chesapeake Bay. The young keeper would come and go on leave throughout the six months following the robberies and murder, periodically returning to his home in south Baltimore.

Despite the passage of time, police continued their analysis of evidence and slowly pieced the crime puzzle together.

On November 26, 1948, six months to the day of the cab driver's death, police finally charged the keeper with murder. The November 27th edition of the *Frederick News* reports, "detectives would not say how they had pieced together the information that led them to arrest [the keeper], 22. Two investigators and a Coast Guard officer went almost 75 miles down Chesapeake Bay Wednesday night and brought [him] back from the

Photo by Bob Trapani, Jr.

A 2000-lb. fog bell, similar to the one that would have been used on Sharkfin Shoal Lighthouse

Sharkfin Shoal Lighthouse off Deal Island, where he was stationed."

The news account went on to state, "He was named in seven separate charges involving the slaying last May 26 of [the cabbie] and the robbery and shooting six days earlier of ..., another cab driver. [The keeper] was held without bail pending a hearing."

On December 15, 1948, the *Frederick News* reported that the lightkeeper was charged with first-degree murder following his acknowledgement of the crimes while on the witness stand. [The young keeper] informed the court that he committed the crimes in order to obtain money to pay for an operation his wife needed.

The keeper further claimed that the shooting death of the second cab driver was an accident. In fact, it was brought to light that the accused was relieved when authorities came to Sharkfin Shoal Lighthouse on Thanksgiving Eve to apprehend him. The keeper's attorney was quoted as asking him: "This matter had been preying on your mind for a long time?"

Following the accused's testimony and deliberation, a three-judge court returned the verdict of first-degree murder, which meant that the lightkeeper faced either death by hanging or life imprisonment for the crimes. His attorney indicated that he might file a motion for a new trial, which prompted the judges to delay imposing the final sentence. During the trial, news reports stated that the accused "sat with bowed head, appearing almost asleep, as the State presented its case against him. He was still huddled over as he testified."

The three-judge panel eventually did deliver a death penalty sentence for the crime of first-degree murder while the convicted keeper was in prison. But two years later William Preston Lane, Jr., governor of Maryland, lifted the death sentence. The governor reduced the severity of the sentence to life imprisonment, stating, "Under all of the circumstances of this case, while I condemn him for the crime that he committed, I will not sign his death warrant."

Governor Lane went on to note, "When arrested, [he] promptly and freely confessed his guilt," Lane said. "I am advised by his spiritual advisors that while confined in the death house, his attitude has been one of deep regret and atonement." In a prepared statement, the governor went on to cite the keeper's background, "He was the fifth of 11 children. He worked after school to help the family. Failing his sophomore year of high school, he joined the Navy at 17. [He] was on an LST at Omaha Beach and Normandy Beach. Once at Norfolk he was docked for being AWOL eight hours. Trial was called off, after a man fell off the dock and [he] saved him from drowning."

In closing, Governor Lane stated, "Notwithstanding the enormity of the crime he has committed, the record does not show [him] to be a confirmed, vicious criminal. In the scales of ultimate justice, it seems to me that the fact that a man has led a creditable life should have some weight, and there is no time that he needs that credit more than when he is faced with punishment by death."

The governor's actions would seem to have brought public closure to the keeper's situation, where he would now serve out the rest of life in prison, but such was not the case. The March 18, 1961, edition of the *Salisbury Times* finds the convict back in the news. While serving his life term at Poplar Hill Correctional Farm in Maryland, the former lighthouse keeper was reported missing. The circumstances surrounding his escape from the correctional facility are not clear, but 40 minutes later he was back in custody.

The *Salisbury Times* reported that the convicted keeper "was found walking along the long lane leading from the Quantico Road into the correctional camp, according to James E. Curran, state superintendent of prisons." The news account went on to state, " 'He was apparently returning to the camp when officers found him,' Mr. Curran said. [The former keeper]...is serving a life term for murder, authorities said."

Author's note: The names of the individuals involved have been omitted in consideration of their families.

Sharkfin Shoal Lighthouse Facts & Figures

1887—The *Annual Report of the Light-House Board* noted that "Shark Fin Shoal, to take the place of Clay Island Light-house, entrance to Fishing Bay and Nanticoke River, Maryland—The site of Clay Island Light-house is being rapidly washed away, to prevent which, expensive works of protection would be needed. The structure is old and in need of repairs almost to the extent of rebuilding. The Board is of the opinion that a light would be of much more service to the interests of navigation if located on Shark Fin Shoal, and therefore recommends that a screw-pile light-house and a fog-signal be built there at an estimated cost of $25,000."

1891—The *Annual Report of the Light-House Board* noted that "This new structure, designed to take the place of the Clay Island light-house, is now in readiness for transportation to the site. It will probably be in position and ready for lighting by September 15, 1891."

1893—The *Annual Report of the Light-House Board* noted that "The light-house was completed early in July, and the light was exhibited August 1, 1892."

1893—Sharkfin Shoal Lighthouse was dark for nearly a week during January as ice—a foot thick on the bay—stopped shipping in its tracks. The *Baltimore Sun* reported on January 20, 1893, that "It is feared that Captain Cole, the keeper, who is alone, has either perished from cold and hunger or is too ill to perform his duties." Once the ice floes started to break-up and run, residents on Maryland's Eastern Shore saw the light from Sharkfin Shoal shining again. The reason for the light being darkened during the period of deep freeze on the bay went unexplained.

1899—The U.S. Lighthouse Service Light List described the lighthouse as a "White hexagonal screw-pile structure; piles and roof, brown; lantern, black; window shutters, green."

1936—The *United States Lighthouse Service Light List* recorded that Sharkfin Shoal Lighthouse showed a fixed white light with a red sector. The light was listed as shining 44 feet above high water, and could be seen 12 nautical miles (the red sector could be seen 9 nautical miles). The station was equipped with a bell for a fog signal that sounded a group of 2 strokes every 15 seconds.

1962—The *United States Coast Guard Light List* noted (two years prior to the historic lighthouse being dismantled) that Sharkfin Shoal Lighthouse showed a flashing white light every

10 seconds, with a red sector. The station was still listed as possessing a bell for a fog signal, which sounded 1 stroke every 20 seconds, continuously from September 15 to June 1.

1964—The lighthouse was dismantled as part of the Coast Guard's effort to modernize aids to navigation and was replaced with a contemporary tower.

1997—The *U.S. Coast Pilot* notes that "Sharkfin Shoal Light, 44 feet above the water, is shown from a skeleton tower with a black and white diamond-shaped daymark." The publication goes on to state that, "In 1978, a partially submerged wreck was reported about 0.2 mile north-northwest of Sharkfin Shoal Light."

Location of former light station: Stood in Fishing Bay between Bishops Head and Deal Island and marked the entrances to the Nanticoke and Wicomico Rivers.

Photo by Bob Trapani, Jr.

Sharps Island Lighthouse
Maryland

Bob Trapani, Jr.

Ice Floes Forever Scar Light Station

Ice has a long history as a dreaded nemesis to the lighthouses of the Chesapeake Bay, but nowhere was the destructive power of winter's annual glacier fields more exacting than Sharps Island Light Station, located south of Tilghman Island. A total of three light stations have stood guard near the entrance to the Choptank River, though the seascape has been greatly altered following years of erosion.

The first lighthouse was a two-story wood dwelling surmounted with a lantern that was physically situated on Sharps Island, an island that at the time the lighthouse was constructed consisted of nearly 400 acres of soft sand and marsh. Today, a few rocks revealed only at extreme low tide are all that remain of what was once a huge island in the middle of the Chesapeake Bay. The erosion dilemma was so severe and unrelenting that it caused the United States Lighthouse Service to establish a screwpile lighthouse offshore of the ever-vanishing Sharps Island in 1865.

The second lighthouse, a quaint white cottage resting on iron pilings enabled the government to conquer the problem of erosion that was ultimately responsible for destroying the original beacon by devouring the land upon which it sat, but its relocation out in the bay only subjected the new structure to another menacing threat—ice floes.

A mere 15 years would pass before the screwpile Sharps Island Lighthouse encountered a dire plight that would forever doom the beacon to a watery grave. The winter of 1880-81 was particularly harsh, with sustained cold temperatures creating a thick layer of ice atop the Chesapeake Bay. Once temperatures moderated enough to break up the frozen mass, the ice floes began to "run" hard on the shoulders of the daily tides.

Unaware of the irreversible consequences posed by the pressing floes against the spindly piling foundation of Sharps Island Lighthouse—its keepers, head keeper Christopher Columbus Butler and assistant Charles L. Tarr—set about their daily duties at dawn on February 10, 1881, as a powerful storm blew a gale across the bay. The storm's mighty winds undoubtedly helped drive great piles of "pancaked" ice up against the light's vulnerable foundation, eventually inflicting fatal force on the iron pilings.

Without warning, several critical foundation supports gave way under the strain of the moving glaciers, causing the ill-fated dwelling and its keepers to be thrown into the icy chaos flowing strongly up bay.

The ensuing moments must have been nothing short of horrifying for keepers Butler and Tarr. First the men endured the terribly frightening experience of being inside a house that is suddenly tossed into the water, causing them and all the dwelling's contents to be thrown to the floor and up against the walls of the structure. Then, after picking themselves off the floor and regaining their senses, the keepers realized they were afloat—but for how long was a question that must have jolted their minds.

Sharps Island Lighthouse was equipped with two small boats, but when the dwelling was unceremoniously cast in the bay, one of the dories broke free and was lost. The combination of the incoming tide and the strong winds spawned by the southeast gale did not allow much time for the two keepers to assess their dreadful dilemma as the stricken lighthouse floated precariously up bay toward Tilghman Island.

Another concern for keepers Butler and Tarr to ponder as the wooden cottage dipped and turned atop the icy swells, was a collision.

What ship in the bay would be on the lookout for a runaway lighthouse with no steering?

Worse yet, fog concealed the hazard posed by the seagoing beacon to shipping—and for that matter, the lives of the apprehensive keepers on board.

Pat Vojtech, author of the book *Lighting the Bay: Tales of Chesapeake Lighthouse*, describes the ensuing harrowing events, stating, "throughout the day and late into the night, the house floated in the freezing water amid heavy floes of ice, which often piled up against the building, and swamped it during the wild, five-mile journey." Vojtech further notes, "somehow, the wooden structure managed to stay afloat until one o'clock the next morning, when it finally grounded in twelve feet of water in Paw Paw Cove, off the west side of Tilghman Island."

After being afloat for sixteen-and-a-half hours, keepers Butler and Tarr were able to leave what now was fast becoming a doomed hulk slowly succumbing to the unforgiving power of the Chesapeake Bay. At any time during their petrifying journey, the lightkeepers could have left their post and attempted to escape in the one remaining boat attached to the lighthouse, but the men chose instead to honorably stand by the stricken beacon and protect its valuable contents. Even when firmly aground, the exhausted keepers remained at their post throughout the night until the next morning, when they finally rowed ashore. Throughout the entire 16-hour, life-threatening experience, the keepers also coped with winter's frigid temperatures without the benefit of a warm fire.

Photo courtesy of Jeremy D'Entremont

Historic image of Sharps Island Lighthouse

F. J. Higginson, Inspector of the Fifth District for the U.S. Lighthouse Service, demonstrated his admiration for the actions of keepers Christopher Columbus Butler and Charles L. Tarr by reporting the incident in glowing fashion to the Lighthouse Board. Higginson urged the Board to issue letters of commendation to both men, citing the fact that, "the keeper and assistant clung to the fallen house.... For sixteen and a half hours, their danger was very great, being in the midst of heavy flowing ice, which would often pile upon the house and thereafter swamp it."

Ten years later, the July 29, 1891, edition of the *Indiana County Gazette* recounted the Sharps Island catastrophe in a feature story entitled "Lighthouse Keeper," and pointing out "an instance of heroism" that occurred the frigid day of February 10, 1881. The news account went on to describe the actions of keepers Butler and Tarr once the lighthouse came to halt full of water, stating, "being satisfied that it would not float off again, the two keepers went ashore in their boat, and when the tide had fallen they returned, saved and took to shore the lens, its pedestal, the oil, the library, much damaged by water, and even the empty oil cans."

Despite the heroics of its keepers, there was no hope of salvaging the doomed Sharps Island Lighthouse. Though still standing somewhat upright in the days following its grounding at high tide during the overnight hours of February 11th, the cottage was firmly held in the clutches of the bay and submerged to its roof, eventually splitting apart from the destructive force of the tides and wind-driven waves.

The runaway lighthouse episode may have come to a conclusion, but that was hardly a consolation to those in the U.S. Lighthouse Service, who knew all too well that without a beacon to warn mariners of the dangers lurking at Sharps Island, a disaster could befall an unsuspecting vessel at any time. Their fears were realized—though, thankfully, without loss of life—as a steamer grounded on Sharps Island two days after ice removed the screwpile lighthouse off its foundation.

One year later, in 1882, the third Sharps Island Lighthouse was lit for the first time, but instead of the structure being of the vulnerable screwpile construction, the U.S. Lighthouse Service established a more rugged caisson lighthouse in hopes that the stout beacon would better endure the scourge of ice floes.

For nearly a century of service, the caisson lighthouse at Sharps Island indeed stood strong in the face of winter's dreaded ice season—until the harsh winter of 1976-77. The lighthouse, now automated, bowed to the force of the frigid floes, which caused the beacon to incur a lean of approximately 15 to 20 degrees. Despite the lean, the lighthouse has continued to serve as aid to navigation, but the combination of it being off-kilter and ongoing deterioration to the structure threatens, eventually, to push the mighty beacon beneath the waves to a watery grave.

Sharps Island Lighthouse Facts & Figures

1838—The original Sharps Island Lighthouse was constructed on Sharps Island itself, which sat in the middle of the Chesapeake Bay off Tilghman Island. The lighthouse, which consisted of a lantern surmounting the keeper's house, was located on the north end of the island, marking the entrance to Choptank River and was lit for the first time in September 1838.

1865—The *Annual Report of the Light-House Board* notes, "(With) the gradual washing away of the ground on which the old light-house at Sharp's Island is built, it became necessary to remove all the furniture from it, including the illuminating apparatus. Hence, from the 1st to the 15th of November, 1865, no light was exhibited from this point. Meanwhile, a tripod of wood-work was constructed, and a steamer's lens established on it which was exhibited on the night of the 16th of December. This temporary appliance will be continued until the new tower now in progress is finished."

1866—The second lighthouse at Sharps Island was a white screwpile structure equipped with a fifth order lens that showed a fixed white light to mariners seeking the entrance to the Choptank River.

1879—The *Annual Report of the Light-House Board* notes, "This light-house suffered somewhat from the heavy drift of the ice during the past winter. Two of the diagonal cast-iron braces were carried away; one tension-brace was broken and one of the horizontal beams bent. The damage was repaired, and to provide against further damage by the ice, a detached ice-breaker was placed about 200 feet to the south of the light-house, in the axis of the current—the direction from which the heavy ice came in 1877 and 1879.

1881—The *Annual Report of the Light-House Board* notes, "By a heavy run of ice on February 10, this light-house was torn from its foundation and carried away; there was no loss of life; the keepers remained on the wreck until it grounded; their conduct is highly commended. The attention of Congress was at once called to the necessity of re-establishing this important light, and on March 3 an appropriation of $35,000 was made for rebuilding the light-house. Deeming an ordinary screw-pile light-house at this place liable to be again destroyed by the heavy runs of ice so prevalent in Chesapeake Bay in severe winters, it was determined to use a cast-iron caisson filled with concrete and surmounted by a tower, also of coast-iron, with a brick lining. The solidity and great weight of such a structure it is thought will be effective. The manufacture has already been commenced under contract by the Builders' Iron Company, of Providence, R.I., under the supervision of the engineer of the Third Light-house District."

1882—The present caisson lighthouse was built to mark the shoal at Sharps Island and first lit on February 1, 1882. According to lighthouse historian F. Ross Holland, the lighthouse was the second caisson ever established on the Chesapeake Bay. The *Annual Report of the Light-House Board* notes, "the structure is an iron tower, 37 feet in height, resting on an iron caisson, 30 feet in diameter and 30 feet in height, filled with concrete. It shows a fixed white light of the fourth order, 55 feet above mean low water.... The new house is so located that a vessel can run a straight course from Sharp's Island Light to Choptank River Light."

1900—By the turn of the 20th century, only 94 acres remained of Sharps Island, which is believed to have measured nearly 1,000 acres in the 1600s.

1904—The April 23rd edition of the *Denton Journal*, Md., notes, "Capt. Christopher Columbus Butler, keeper of the Bloody Point Lighthouse, Chesapeake Bay, has resigned after 25 years service.

Capt. Butler was well-known among the watermen of the Chesapeake and its tributaries. He was keeper of Sharp's Island Light in 1881, when it was carried away by the ice, but he stayed with the floating wreck and saved the lens and other valuables belonging to the government."

1914—The *U.S. Lighthouse Service Light List* notes that Sharps Island Lighthouse showed a fixed white light with a red sector 54 feet above mean high water. The publication goes on to say the light could be seen 13 nautical miles and the structure described as a brown tower on a cylindrical pier. The lighthouse was equipped with a fog bell that sounded a double-stroke every 10 seconds.

1937—The *U.S. Coast Pilot* notes that "Sharps Island, a low island marked by a single tree, lies in Chesapeake Bay...the island is subject to rapid erosion."

1961—The *U.S. Coast Pilot* notes that "Sharps Island Light is 3 miles due east of a point 106 miles along Chesapeake Bay main channel from the Virginia Capes. Tiny Sharps Island, 1.3 miles south-southeast of the light, is subject to rapid erosion. Just south of the island is a small Naval danger zone."

1977—After ice floes caused the lighthouse to lean, the fourth order Fresnel lens was removed and replaced with a 250mm plastic lens that was attached to a plate on the light's structure. Author Pat Vojtech captures the significance of this event, stating, "Sharps Island Lighthouse—the leaning tower of the Chesapeake—is the only caisson ever moved by ice in the Bay."

2006—Sharps Island Lighthouse remains an active aid to navigation and is maintained by the United States Coast Guard.

Photo by Shirin Pagels

Smith Point Lighthouse
Virginia

Bob Trapani, Jr.

Termites Invade Chesapeake Bay Light

Of the five lighthouses that have stood sentinel on or near Smith Point since 1802, the least likely structure to endure the wrath of hungry wood-eating termites would be the last beacon built at the light station site south of the Potomac River in 1897. The imposing 52-foot cast-iron caisson, with its octagonal brick superstructure, stands 2.5 miles east-southeast of Smith Point, and one would naturally presume out of reach of even the most industrious clan of termites.

On May 23, 1970, the *Sheboygan Press* in Wisconsin noted that "the idea of a band of termites manning an amphibious landing craft or dropping from a plane in an airborne assault is a pretty ridiculous one. But, however, they did it, an invasion force of termites made it from the Virginia mainland to a lonely lighthouse in Chesapeake Bay." The United States Coast Guard countered by calling in "tactical" reinforcements in the form of the Atlanta-based Orkin Exterminating Company to do battle with the band of renegade wood-eating insects.

When the termite damage was initially discovered, the lighthouse keepers believed that the cause of deterioration was from dry rot; however, a professional analysis dispelled this notion. Entomologist Dr. John Osmun of Purdue University confirmed that the damage to a wooden floor, wall and baseboard on the third level of Smith Point Lighthouse was caused by the ravaging presence of termites despite the fact that the discovery confounded everything known about termites.

How an army of termites managed to invade the water-locked sentinel was beyond even the explanation of the expert entomologists, who tackled the dilemma, but one thing is certain—the colony's troublesome handiwork was real and it threatened to undermine the interior of the historic structure. The *Sheboygan Press* theorized that "in addition to being far from the nearest dry land, the 74-year-old lighthouse is surrounded by sea water with an average depth of 17 feet and was erected on a concrete caisson sunk 40 feet into the bay bottom." The newspaper account went on to say, "that appeared to rule out any possibility of the termites tunneling two and half miles from land to the site."

Aside from the site's distance from land and stout exterior of cast-iron and brick, another fascinating factor that perplexed the experts hired to eradicate the insects was that termites require fresh water to survive. How the colony thrived in a saltwater environment was yet another mystery associated with their presence on the lighthouse. The news report noted that "extermination experts believe the termites either flew or were blown to the lighthouse, or they were carried aboard with supplies for the Coastguardsmen."

The lighthouse keepers may not have been aware of just how the wood-eating pests invaded their offshore home, but they were certainly happy to rid themselves of the castaways.

Photo courtesy of the U.S. Coast Guard

The fourth Smith Point Lighthouse, built in 1868, was a screwpile style structure. It was destroyed by ice in 1895.

The Orkin Exterminating Company used a one-two punch of chemical spray and liquid fumigant to overwhelm the termites, thus ending the unexpected siege. The *Sheboygan Press* concluded their report by stating, "The termites are gone now and nobody is expecting their return—so long as there is some wood to tap for good luck."

Smith Point Lighthouse Facts & Figures

1802—The first Smith Point Lighthouse was established on land. Five years later, a hurricane caused extensive damage to the structure, requiring it to be rebuilt in 1807. Severe erosion then undermined the structure and in 1828, the lighthouse was rebuilt for the third time.

1868—The fourth Smith Point Lighthouse was a screw-pile structure built offshore and lit for the first time on September 9, 1868. The lightkeepers abandoned this structure during the severe winter of 1893, when ice floes threatened to topple the cottage from its pile foundation. Two years later, "Old Man Winter" claimed victory when the ravaging ice floes carried away the helpless lighthouse on February 14, 1895.

1897—The fifth, and present, Smith Point Lighthouse, was constructed and lit for the first time on October 15, 1897. The beacon was automated in November 1971.

The *United States Lighthouse Service Light List* described Smith Point Lighthouse as showing a flashing white light every 10 seconds with red sector and a radio beacon. The structure is listed as being located in 19 feet of water, on the south side of the entrance to the Potomac River. The publication further notes that a fourth order light shows 52 feet above the water and can be seen 13 nautical miles. A diaphone fog signal sounds once every 15 seconds.

1997—The *U.S.Coast Pilot* describes the structure as "a white square brick tower and octagonal dwelling on a brown cylindrical pier."

Photo courtesy of the U.S. Coast Guard

Thimble Shoal Lighthouse

Virginia

Collisions & Fire Haunt Offshore Light

Imagine living in a dwelling where terror was a nemesis that could not be warded off. Whether hiding under a cloak of darkness or using the element of quiet surprise in broad daylight, the inescapable cloud of horror was always nearby, threatening to strike a fatal blow of cataclysmic proportions with nary a warning. One such place proved to be the offshore light station at Thimble Shoal in Chesapeake Bay.

Every offshore lighthouse in the Chesapeake has possessed some sort of inherent hazardous element throughout its service, but no bay beacon was more fraught with a history of terrifying danger than "The Thimble," as it was known to its keepers and mariners. The plight of Thimble Shoal, with its litany of harrowing collisions and fires, comes as no surprise when considering the shoal the beacon stands guard over, as well as its close proximity to the shipping channel.

For any vessel entering the mouth of the Chesapeake Bay, the notorious Thimble Shoal Channel is an unavoidable trek along its journey into the bay. The nearly 10-mile stretch that culminates just below the entrance to Hampton Roads might just as well be named the "Channel of Doom," given its penchant for crossing paths with the hands of fate at Thimble Shoal Lighthouse.

As lighthouse author Pat Vojtech notes in her book, *Lighting the Bay: Tales of Chesapeake Lighthouses,* "With collisions occurring almost yearly, it was no wonder that Thimble Shoal became known as the unlucky lighthouse." Vojtech added, "But it is understandable why so many collisions occurred there. Thimble Shoal Lighthouse marks one of the busiest ports on the Bay, second only to Baltimore. Many more vessels pass near the lighthouse than any other lighthouse on the Bay. Thimble Shoal is also the most exposed of all lighthouses in the Chesapeake. Located just twenty miles inside Cape Henry, it gets the full brunt of storms blowing off the open ocean, as well as wave action and currents that are considerably stronger than at most other locations on the Bay."

Regardless of the logical explanations as to why terror's dark shadow hung over Thimble Shoal, the reasoning proved no comfort to the keepers tasked with the duty of manning the perilous light station. Built in 1872, the wooden hexagonal cottage atop screw-pile legs stood peacefully for only eight years before a chain reaction of grim drama took center stage in 1880.

The mystery surrounding a devastating fire that ended up consuming the wood frame structure on October 30, 1880, was never explained.

The official report of the United States Lighthouse Service simply stated that "the origin of the fire was not definitely ascertained." If the lighthouse keepers did know how the blaze took life at Thimble Shoal, no one was saying.

Thanks in part to the light's iron work being primarily intact, rebuilding the lighthouse was less of a dilemma than it normally would have been. Coupled with the iron screw-pile foundation proving sound, was the fact that a similar cottage had been completed for Bells Rock Light at the time of the fire, hence the U.S. Lighthouse Service decided to modify its plans and send the new wood dwelling to Thimble Shoal instead owing to the importance of the light for ships on the bay. After 35 days of furious work, contractors finished the new lighthouse at Thimble Shoal and lit it for the first time on December 24, 1880.

The new 1880 beacon showed a light from a fourth order Fresnel lens at a focal plane of 42 feet, which could be seen by mariners for nearly 12 miles. The U.S. Lighthouse Service added a second fog bell at the station in apparent understanding that the station was situated in harm's way. The huge bells were struck simultaneously at five-second intervals. The hope was that if thick weather concealed the light's guiding beam that the doleful audible gong of the bells would provide the mariner with sufficient warning.

The *1891 U.S. Lighthouse Service Annual Report* was direct and to the point, if not detailed, as to the next disaster that struck Thimble Shoal Light on March 15, 1891. Under the cover of darkness, the report stated, "The light-house was considerably damaged by the running against it of an unknown steamer. One end of the main gallery was badly injured and one of the iron girders was broken. The station was promptly repaired."

The keepers aboard Thimble Shoal, who were no doubt thrust into a state of panic upon the ship's impact, evidently could not obtain a good look at the mystery steamer silhouetted by the realm of nightfall in order to identify it. The rogue steamer left the scene of the accident with apparently no conscience as to the fate of the lightkeepers inside after dealing the structure a heavy blow.

On April 14, 1898, seven years after the lighthouse was first struck by a wayward vessel, a tug and barge loaded with coal was passing Thimble Shoal Lighthouse and heading up the bay. The tug boat managed to round the shoal safely but the barge in tow was not as fortunate. Whether powerful currents or pilot error is to blame, one thing is certain—"The Thimble" absorbed a crushing blow that sent its keepers reeling.

Image courtesy of the U.S. Coast Guard

This sketch of the original screwpile-style Thimble Shoal Lighthouse, built in 1872, shows a very different structure when compared to the present day, caisson-style light, which was completed in 1914.

The *1898 U.S. Lighthouse Service Annual Report* described the vicious collision, noting, "The entire lower gallery on the southeast side was carried away and the two adjoining sides were damaged. All the joists in the southeast section were broken and thrust out of position."

The report went on to say, "The lower socket casting on the south-by-east corner was badly cracked, and the 5-inch horizontal brace on the southeast side was bent about five inches out of line, Other parts of the ironworks suffered, and the house was lifted about one-half inch off the radial beams. The shock also broke the pinion of the revolving machinery of the lens."

The lighthouse service reported to Congress that repairs to the cottage dwelling would be carried out quickly as possible. In addition, unlike the 1891 collision where the keepers were unable to identify the sea-going culprit, the men on board Thimble Shoal at the time of the crash were apparently able to do so this time around, for the lighthouse service cites the fact that "reimbursement will be demanded of the company owning the barge."

Photo courtesy of the U.S. Coast Guard

The caisson foundation for the new Thimble Shoal Lighthouse is seen on the left, with the remains of the former screwpile light, at right. The contractors building the new lighthouse maintained a temporary wooden shack for workers atop the old light's skeleton foundation.

Though Thimble Shoal Lighthouse managed to survive the 1891 collision, the hands of fate would exact their revenge on the helpless structure two days after Christmas on December 27, 1909. Any remnants of Christmas spirit present at the lighthouse on this portentous day were instantly transformed into a desperate fight for life amidst the chaos of splintered timbers and raging flames. The four-masted schooner *Malcolm Baxter, Jr.* bludgeoned Thimble Shoal Lighthouse with such force that the wooden cottage dwelling was nearly severed in two pieces.

The massive schooner was sailing up the Chesapeake Bay for Hampton Roads in ballast when a powerful west wind blew across the Thimble Shoal channel. The captain was unable to maintain a safe course, fighting in vain to remain in the shipping channel. Before long terror gripped the crew as they helplessly watched their vessel head straight for the screw-pile beacon. Moments later, a direct hit was inflicted on the lighthouse.

The *Washington Post* described the scene, noting, "The house crumbled before the vessel like a box, and in the smash-up the stove in the lighthouse was overturned, setting the building on fire." The news account went on to say, "Seeing that the flames must destroy the building, the lighthouse men lowered a lifeboat and set out for shore."

Three keepers were on duty at Thimble Shoal when the horrifying collision and ensuing fire turned their world upside down. Two men, keeper Joseph B. Thomas and assistant Isaac D. Wells, Jr., spent their initial moments following the collision trying frantically to douse the flames enveloping the kitchen floor after the overturned stove threw hot coals across the room. Despite being surrounded by water, the keepers were unable to make any headway against the fast-moving blaze. Seeing that their efforts were futile, Thomas and Wells ran outside to the light's skiff, lowered it to the water and retreated away from the building inferno.

In the meantime, as the two keepers rowed quickly away from the lighthouse, another assistant was even in more dire straits up in the lantern of the light where he was nearly killed upon impact by the gorging jib boom of the *Malcolm Baxter, Jr.*

In her book *Lighting the Bay: Tales of Chesapeake Lighthouses*, author Pat Vojtech describes the chaotic scene that unfolded at the top of the structure, saying, "Inside the beacon, the open flame of the light had just been extinguished. It was 8:30 a.m., an hour after sunrise, and assistant keeper Thomas L. Fulcher was in the lantern room at the top of the lighthouse, cleaning the lens."

Vojtech goes on to say, "Fulcher had the lens in his arms, polishing it, when the flying jib boom of Baxter shot through the lantern gallery, shattering glass everywhere and knocking him off his feet." Fulcher picked himself off the floor laden with shattered glass and bolted down the winding wood steps that led from the lantern to the first level of the lighthouse. Seeing the living quarters being devoured by flames, Fulcher made fast for the door outside to escape the unquenchable fire.

Amazingly, no one died in this terrible accident. The *Malcolm Baxter, Jr.* was able to break free of the lighthouse after a northwest wind pivoted the injured vessel and allowed it to retreat from the intense heat, smoke and flames. Another vessel in the area—the *John Twohy*, observed the flames engulfing the

Photo courtesy of the U.S. Coast Guard

The present day Thimble Shoal Lighthouse, on left, during the days when keepers manned the beacon. The skeletal legs that once supported the old screwpile lighthouse stand off to the right in this photograph.

lighthouse and immediately came to the scene where they were able to pluck the lightkeepers from the water where they were eventually taken to shore at Old Point. The *Malcolm Baxter, Jr.* was then taken in tow to Norfolk for repairs.

As for the Thimble Shoal Lighthouse, the fire had devoured the wooden structure in no time at all, thus necessitating the United States Lighthouse Service to establish a lightship at the site until yet another sentinel could be rebuilt at the dangerous location. Five years would pass before a new lighthouse was lit at Thimble Shoal, but this time, a more stout structure was established.

Rather than replacing the charred remains atop the scorched screw-pile foundation with another wooden cottage, the lighthouse service elected to construct a cast-iron caisson lighthouse adjacent to the former beacon.

During the construction process, the dreaded fear of ongoing collisions at the light station site did not cease. On November 25, 1911, the tug *Prudence* and a barge in tow slammed into the iron screw-pile foundation that once supported the wooden cottage and subsequently twisted some of the piles. The new caisson foundation for Thimble Shoal Lighthouse wasn't yet complete when it too was struck by passing vessels. A barge being towed by the tug *Kenmore* crashed into the light station on April 11, 1913, followed by the barge *B. Mohawk* in tow of the tug *Virginia*, which struck the site on May 10, 1914.

Even when the 55-foot tall caisson lighthouse was finished and first lit on December 1, 1914, accidents continued to occur at the station.

Three-and-a-half months after the new lighthouse was placed into service, the massive six-masted schooner, *Addie M. Lawrence,* struck the lighthouse, and on September 24, 1916, another unidentified barge in tow of a tug rammed the old light's twisted screw-pile foundation. For the keepers of Thimble Shoal Lighthouse, life was never free of the worry that in a moment's notice their whole world could be turned upside down. The lighthouse was automated in 1964.

In addition to the ice floes that destroyed the original Thimble Shoal Lighthouse, the station and the shoal itself have a long history of tragedy, heroism and mystery.

Thimble Shoal Lighthouse Facts & Figures

1872—The *New York Herald* printed a "Notice to Mariners" on October 22, 1872, stating, "The screw pile lighthouse on Thimble Shoals, which has been christened the 'Bug Light,' is in successful operation and the old Willoughby Spit Light has been withdrawn and the position marked by a black buoy."

1880—The screwpile lighthouse was destroyed by a fire of unknown origin on Oct. 30, 1880. Due to its critical importance to navigation, the United States Lighthouse Service expedited the process of rebuilding the light. Thirty-five days later, on Christmas Eve, Thimble Shoal Lighthouse was relit on Dec. 24, 1880.

1891—An unidentified steamer collided with the wooden lighthouse and caused extensive damage

1898—A wayward tug and barge carrying coal struck the lighthouse on April 14, 1898, inflicting serious damage on the structure.

1908—The *Washington Post* reported on January 28, 1908, "The barge *Mascot,* from Baltimore to Norfolk, went down in the Chesapeake Bay before last midnight. All aboard the vessel, the master, the wife and child, and the master's mate were rescued by the keeper of the Thimble Lighthouse just before the barge went down. They are now at the lighthouse. The lighthouse keeper proved himself a hero in making the rescue. The barge was a mile away from the lighthouse. The keeper seeing the immediate peril of those aboard rowed to the barge over the stormy sea and took them off."

1909—A schooner being towed by a tug rammed the lighthouse on December 27, 1909, causing considerable damage to the structure before a fire, started from the dwelling's stove being overturned by the impact of the collision, completely consumed the wooden lighthouse.

1914—The *Lighthouse Service Bulletin* noted that "Thimble Shoal Light Station, Va.: Light and fog signal went into commission December 1."

1915—The schooner *Addie M. Lawrence* struck the caisson lighthouse on March 6.

1918—The *Lighthouse Service Bulletin* noted that, "On August 1 H. C. Groom, keeper, and Benjamin D. Preston, second assistant keeper, of Thimble Shoal Light Station, Va., went to the assistance of a disabled motor boat with six persons aboard, about one-half mile from the station, and towed it to Hampton Creek, where the occupants landed safely."

1920—The *Lighthouse Service Bulletin* noted that "The severe storm which prevailed along the Middle and North Atlantic coasts early in February resulted in considerable damage to lighthouse property, and caused two light vessels to break from their moorings...(later) On February 4, the heavy seas striking Thimble Shoal Light Station, Chesapeake Bay, carried away the station motor boat and boat davits, and broke two port glasses in the basement and a portion of the deck. The motor boat was later recovered at Ocean View, where it had been washed ashore.

1964—Thimble Shoal Lighthouse was automated. The light remains an active aid to navigation today.

Photo by Bob Trapani, Jr.

Thomas Point Shoal Lighthouse

Maryland

Bob Trapani, Jr.

Light Station Goes Toe to Toe with Mother Nature

Today's gorgeous screwpile light with its distinctive red and white snug cottage, is the icon of Chesapeake Bay, but what some people do not realize is that this offshore structure was not the first Thomas Point Shoal Lighthouse. The original sentinel was a 30-foot-tall, granite tower established on shore in 1825. The light station, which included a small keeper's house, was constructed by John Donohoo, the famous lighthouse builder, who is credited with erecting at least 13 other Chesapeake Bay beacons.

Very little is known about the first light station, but what is known is that the beacon, which was built near the edge of the bay south of Annapolis on Thomas Point, was in a fight for its existence not long after being first commissioned. The insatiable tides of the bay wasted little time in thwarting the well being of the granite tower. In only 15 years, the scouring effects of massive ice floes, inundating storm surge and the ebb and flow of the daily tides had devoured the soft clay bank that once safely kept the Thomas Point Light from the destructive reaches of the sea.

The man in charge of America's lighthouses at the time—Stephen Pleasonton, the Fifth Auditor of the Treasury (1820-52)—summed up the dilemma of the original Thomas Point Shoal Light in a letter to the Honorable John P. Kennedy, chairman of the House of Representatives Committee on Commerce.

In his letter, Pleasonton stated, "This light was placed upon a clay bank at least 30 feet high, and about 500 feet from the water. Such was the action of the water upon the bank that in a few years it was washed away to within 50 feet of the light, upon being informed of which, I directed a quantity of rubble stone to be placed at the base of the bank."

Pleasonton went on to state, "This arrested the water but in a slight degree, and in 1838 it had approached within 15 feet of the lighthouse when I contracted with Winslow Lewis to take down the tower and rebuild it in a secure place for $2,000."

What Pleasonton's letter does not state is the questionable qualifications of his friend, Winslow Lewis, as a contractor. None of the lights constructed by Lewis were of lasting quality, and the second Thomas Point Shoal Lighthouse would be no exception. After taking down the original 30-foot tower, Lewis directed his crew to rebuild a new light tower, using some of the granite from the dismantled beacon, behind the keeper's dwelling.

Lewis gives no reason for the rationale of constructing the new lighthouse directly behind the keepers house, but in doing so he was required to raise the height of the beacon by at least three feet in order for its light to be seen above the roof of the dwelling. The U.S. Treasury may have thought at the time that it received a "bargain" at $2,000 with Lewis' quote to construct the lighthouse, but his suspect workmanship ensured the government got what they paid for. In this particular case, the results were less than desirable.

By 1872, the United States Lighthouse Service (USLHS) stepped up its efforts to petition Congress for the funds to replace the dilapidated beacon built by Lewis. The combination of bad workmanship and the one-two punch of storm winds and driving rain had exacted their unforgiving toll on the structure. In the *Annual Report* for that year, the USLHS bemoaned the terrible condition of the lighthouse, stating, "The rain, in windy weather, beats through the old masonry of the tower, flooding the inside of the structure, and frequently damaging the material in charge of the keeper."

The keeper's miserable conditions and the anxieties over the tower's structural integrity were not the only concerns. Mariners were also voicing their displeasure in relation to the effectiveness of the lighthouse to protect them from the dreaded shoals lurking just over a mile offshore. Neither the light, which was hardly in an advantageous position situated on land, or its ineffective fog bell, was much help at safeguarding ships calling on the Port of Baltimore. The *1872 Annual Report* noted that, "Its present location is such that little use can be made of it at night, and in times of foggy or thick weather it is utterly useless."

The third, and present-day, Thomas Point Shoal Lighthouse was built in 1875 and consists of a screwpile foundation with a two-story wooden cottage surmounted by a lantern. Once established, the beacon on land at Thomas Point was discontinued, but left standing in place. The new lighthouse was equipped at the time with a 3-order Fresnel lens, and it showed a red flash every 20 seconds from a focal plane of 43 feet.

Unlike the previous two shore-side Thomas Point Shoal light stations that coped with steadily advancing erosion, the new offshore beacon would wage an ongoing battle with Mother Nature in the open waters of the Chesapeake Bay. Like all screwpile lighthouses built on the bay, the structure was extremely vulnerable to a dreaded winter nemesis—ice. Just over a year after the station was established massive ice floes would put the structural integrity of Thomas Point Shoal Lighthouse to the supreme test.

As head keeper Eugene Burchenal and a young laborer by the name of George A. Miller went about their duties on the frigid morning of January 17, 1877, the frozen mass imprisoning the lighthouse was about to make a "run." Keeper Burchenal's official report to the Fifth District Inspector states what happened

Photo by Bob Trapani, Jr.

next at the helpless site. Burchenal noted that, "I regret to report that the ice came down on the house in very heavy fields at 9 o'clock a.m. on the morning of the 17th. Some of the ice over 2 feet thick presing (sic) the house back and on the rebound snaped (sic) the cast iron cap."

While the keepers concerned themselves with whether the mighty ice fields would destroy the beacon's screwpile foundation and throw it down, the structure continued to vibrate and shake horribly in the face of each crushing movement of the floes that were riding the shoulders of the morning tide. Before long, the keepers were alarmed at the sound of glass crashing to the floor. Racing topside, the keepers must have stood aghast at the site of the beacon's precious Fresnel lens shattered in pieces upon the floor, not to mention the sudden threat of fire as oil from the light spilled everywhere.

Keeper Burchenal noted the disaster in his report, stating, "At the same time (that the ice pressing against the screwpile foundation in frightening fashion) the lens was turned over and broken to pieces, the two hundred gallon oil buts was turned over and the oil spread all over the house."

As the keeper's report stated, the men anticipated that the continual shock of the ice floes, slamming against the structure, might cause harm to the lens, and therefore took the precaution of attempting to secure it. "We had the lens lashed with back stays through the ventilators to the railing of the balcony," says Burchenal, but "it was no use. Nothing could stand that shaking up. I will try to stick to the house until further orders.... Will burn fixed white light in Solar Lamp until I get other orders."

Apparently, keeper Eugene Burchenal was not satisfied with the emergency lamp that was deployed in place of the broken Fresnel lens. The beacon's significantly reduced intensity must have created a great concern for the safety of shipping since he risked his personal welfare to row across the Chesapeake Bay to the old lighthouse on Thomas Point. In doing so the keeper accepted the fact that the bay was fraught with the immense hazard to his small boat and him as mini glaciers floated precariously atop the entire icy seascape.

In any event, Keeper Burchenal's efforts were both selfless and courageous, exemplifying the type of dedication many keepers of the USLHS exhibited time and again as they sought to protect their fellow man at sea. Sandy Clunies, a certified genealogist and the historian for the Chesapeake Chapter of the United States Lighthouse Society, takes a deeper look at the actions of Eugene Burchenal.

In her observation, Ms. Clunies states, "Keeper Burchenal's report only hints at the dangerous drama that unfolded at the Thomas Point Shoal Lighthouse that night. He was steadfast in the turmoil, and his decisions demonstrate that the need for the light was uppermost in his thoughts." Clunies goes on to comment, "The next day, setting aside any concerns for his personal safety, he took a boat through the icy waters back to shore and somehow gathered the supplies and equipment needed to relight the 'old lighthouse' at Thomas Point that have been inactive for at least fourteen months."

The screwpile Thomas Point Shoal Lighthouse withstood the incredible onslaught of the ice fields, and the damage it sustained to the iron pile foundation was repaired soon afterward. The lighthouse was also provided with a new Fresnel lens in place of the original that was shattered by the movement of the ice floes. One notable improvement that was made by the USLHS in the aftermath of this incident was the establishment of a detached icebreaker that was placed in the axis of the current, approximately 90 feet north of the lighthouse.

The *1877 Annual Report*, states the icebreaker consisted of "three wrought-iron screw-piles, connected together by double channel-iron beams,

Photo by Bob Trapani, Jr.

The automated beacon in the Thomas Point Lighthouse is visible for 16 miles.

surmounted by heavy cast-iron caps, securely bolted together." In addition, contractors placed an ample quantity of riprap around the piles for extra protection against future ice floes. The icebreaker remains in place today.

Life at Thomas Point Shoal Lighthouse was relatively calm for the next 31 years, but a severe thunderstorm over the Chesapeake Bay would change all that in a flash on July 25, 1908. The keepers were no doubt hunkered down in the screw-pile cottage as rain fell from a darkened sky periodically lit up in frightening fashion by powerful flashes of lightning. The crackling sound of thunder continued to shake the wooden beacon when suddenly at 1:40 p.m. a stray bolt of lightning scored a direct hit on the defenseless structure.

Though not on duty at the time of the harrowing incident, head keeper H.G. Wingate later reported to the Fifth District Inspector in a letter that "lightning struck the smoke stack of the kitchen and nearly cut it in two and run down and badly tore the kitchen floor up all so (sic) damaged the lightning conductor there was no fire we can not use the stove on account of the stack being damaged."

Fortunately the keepers escaped injury and the lighthouse did not suffer a fire in the wake of nature's electrical nightmare.

Photo courtesy of Henry Gonzalez

Some of the volunteers involved in Thomas Point Lighthouse preservation efforts, shown at the light, include, from left, Cullen Chambers, lead preservationist; Anne Puppa, vice president for preservation; Henry Gonzalez, vice president for East Coast operations; Sandy Clunies, historian; and author Bob Trapani, Jr.

Over the years, many northeast gales and hurricanes have invaded the Chesapeake Bay and tested the durability of Thomas Point Shoal Lighthouse. The most recent meteorological monster to hammer the upper Chesapeake Bay was the frightening remnants of Hurricane Isabel in September 2003. Despite strong winds and destructive storm surge that inundated the shores of Annapolis, Thomas Point Shoal Lighthouse stood strong, losing only the wooden storage deck beneath the cottage. The U.S. Coast Guard later replaced the deck.

Thomas Point Shoal Lighthouse Facts & Figures

1825—The original Thomas Point Shoal Lighthouse was built on shore and stood 30 feet tall, with a small keeper's dwelling. According to the U.S. Coast Guard Historian's Office, "few details exist about this original light. It is assumed it was built of granite quarried in Port Deposit, Md. .... The light stood on a bank overlooking the Chesapeake Bay, approximately 100 feet from the water. The site proved particularly susceptible to shore erosion...by 1838 the water had come to within 15 feet of the tower and plans were made to move it."

1840—Erosion caused a second lighthouse to be built at Thomas Point in 1840. The new tower was constructed using some of the stone from the original lighthouse. The contractor built the new beacon behind the keeper's dwelling and thus raised the height of the structure by three feet than the previous 30-foot tower so that the lantern could clear the keeper's dwelling.

1855—The U.S. Lighthouse Board installed a fifth order Fresnel lens in the beacon.

1875—The present screwpile Thomas Point Shoal Lighthouse was constructed and first lit on November 20, exhibiting a light from a fourth order Fresnel lens. The lighthouse is located offshore in Chesapeake Bay just north of the South River and southward of the City of Annapolis.

1894—The July 11, 1894 edition of the *Frederick News*, Md., reports, "Events of Interest Here and There, Yesterday and

Today.... Four persons were rescued from a capsized boat by the keeper of the Thomas Point Lighthouse."

1905—A letter from keeper JB Suit dated February 26, 1905, to Commander Henry McCrea, USN, Inspector 5th District, Baltimore, Maryland states, "Sir: I am sorry to have to report that the assistant Mr. Peter S. Earle is losing his mind and I can not trust him with the light he has worried me much I think his ease should be looked after I went ashore to the island and got Mr. George Tyler to come out and take him off the station on the 26 Please let me know what to do as I have a very bad cold. Very Respectfully, JB Suit, Keeper"

1907—The February 8, 1907, edition of the *Washington Post* reported a story entitled, "All Night in Open Boat...Lighthouse Attendant Caught in Ice in the Chesapeake." The account states, "Charles Larsen, assistant keeper of the Thomas Point Lighthouse, six miles from Annapolis, was brought here this afternoon with a frostbitten right hand, which he had received while exposed in an open boat on the Chesapeake Bay during the whole of last night. He tried ineffectually to reach Annapolis and was carried across the bay by pack ice. He was rescued by a tug boat."

1914—The U.S. Lighthouse Service Light List notes that Thomas Point Shoal Lighthouse showed a flashing white light every 5 seconds with a red sector. The publication goes on to state that the light was visible for 12 miles from a focal plane of 43-feet and that a fog bell sounded a "triple stroke every 30 seconds."

1916—The August edition of the *Lighthouse Service Bulletin* noted that "On the night of May 23 Sheldon R. Van Houter, keeper of Thomas Point Shoal Light Station, Md., furnished food and dry clothing to the occupant of the gasoline launch *Rex*, which arrived at the light station in a disabled condition. The next day the keeper towed the launch to Annapolis, a distance of 6 miles, where a tug was secured."

1986—Thomas Point Shoal Lighthouse was automated.

2004—On May 1, the U.S. Department of the Interior transferred ownership of Thomas Point Shoal Lighthouse from the Federal government to the new Thomas Point Shoal Lighthouse Public-Private Partnership. The group of new caretakers is comprised of five entities—the United States Lighthouse Society, Chesapeake Chapter of the USLHS, Annapolis Maritime Museum, City of Annapolis and Anne Arundel County, Maryland. In addition to the preservation of Thomas Point Shoal Lighthouse, the partnership intends to open the offshore historic site to the general public for educational tours. The Annapolis Maritime Museum is also serving as a land-base educational facility for Thomas Point Shoal Lighthouse.

2005—The *United States Coast Guard Light List* notes that the Thomas Point Shoal Lighthouse shows a flashing white light every 5 seconds, with two red sectors from a focal plane of 43 feet. The white light is visible 16 nautical miles, with the red sectors visible 11 nautical miles. The lighthouse is also equipped with a fog signal that sounds one blast every 15 seconds.

To learn more about the Thomas Point Shoal Lighthouse
Public-Private Partnership, visit:

www.thomaspointlighthouse.org

Thomas Point Shoal Lighthouse
P.O. Box 5940
Annapolis, MD 21403
Email: info@thomaspointlight.org

Other lighthouse/maritime partners include:
Annapolis Maritime Museum
www.annapolismaritimemuseum.org

United States Lighthouse Society
www.uslhs.org

Chesapeake Chapter of the U.S. Lighthouse Society
www.cheslights.org

Photo by Bob Trapani, Jr.

Turkey Point Lighthouse
Maryland

Bob Trapani, Jr.

United States President Appoints Light Keeper

The appointment of Mrs. Fannie Salter as keeper of Turkey Point Light is not only one of the most historic moments in Chesapeake Bay lighthouse history, but also in America's heritage of keeping a good light burning for the protection of the seafarer. Though there were many lighthouses with female keepers from the early 1800s on, only Mrs. Salter can lay claim to receiving her appointment from the highest office in the Union—the President of the United States.

The story of Fannie's unique distinction and proud service as lightkeeper of the beacon at Turkey Point, which marks the entrance to Maryland's Elk River at the head of the Chesapeake Bay, began when her husband Clarence assumed the duties of keeper on July 25, 1922. Clarence, who was transferring from a light in Virginia, was embarking on a new life at the secluded Maryland station with his wife Fannie and their three children—Mabel, Olga and Bradley, which seemed to suit him just fine.

The Salter family settled in at Turkey Point Light Station, making the normal adjustments to relocating to a new home and life. For Clarence, after spending years of service on the offshore screwpile York Spit Lighthouse away from his family for extended periods of time, obtaining a land-locked station had to be satisfying since it was a duty that he could carry out in the company and love of his family.

Unknown to the Salter's, their peaceful life at Turkey Point would encounter a life-altering experience less than three years later that would greatly impact their family and write a new chapter in the history of U.S. lighthouse history.

In February 1925, keeper Clarence Salter was diagnosed with appendicitis. He subsequently left Turkey Point and was admitted to the government hospital in Baltimore where he underwent emergency surgery—not realizing at the time that he would never return to the lighthouse. An appendectomy was performed in an effort to save the keeper's life, but three days later he died of an embolism. Suddenly Mrs. Salter not only lost her beloved husband, but as a widow with three children, she was also faced with having to leave Turkey Point Lighthouse as well.

Fannie, desiring very much to become the next keeper at the lighthouse, received a meeting with Captain Harold D. King, Superintendent of Lighthouses in Turkey Point's district, and asked for the appointment. Though Captain King, who would eventually succeed George Putnam as Commissioner of the United States Lighthouse Service in 1935, was a kind and understanding man, he was powerless to grant Mrs. Salter her request.

Just a few years prior, the Civil Service Commission passed a ruling barring women from becoming keepers due to concerns over their ability to handle the cumbersome and heavy equipment that was increasingly being put in place at America's light stations.

Heartbroken, Mrs. Salter returned home to Turkey Point with the understanding that she had but 30 days to relocate her family and vacate the quiet light station. Shortly thereafter though, an influential physician and former state senator in North East, the nearest town to Turkey Point, learned of Fannie's plight. He decided to leverage his many contacts in an effort to help. As a result, U.S. Senator O.E. Weller subsequently became involved and during the eleventh hour, as Fannie was resigned to leaving the lighthouse, he was successful in

Photo courtesy of Jeremy D'Entremont

Fanny Salter, keeper at Turkey Point Lighthouse

obtaining an appointment with President Calvin Coolidge.

In what had to be one of the happiest moments in Fannie's life, she learned from her daughter Mabel that President Coolidge overrode the ruling of the Civil Service Commission and granted Mrs. Salter the honor of becoming the next keeper of Turkey Point Light Station. There was no modern precedent for such an appointment occurring by permission of the President of the United States. Though Presidents George Washington and Thomas Jefferson personally appointed various keepers during our nation's infancy, the practice soon ended when the responsibilities of the office became overwhelming.

Fannie, who was acting as temporary keeper until her circumstances were worked out one way or the other, personally documented one of the most unique moments in American lighthouse history when she penned the following entry in the station log on April 1, 1925: "Northwest fresh, cloudy. Received telegram that I have been appointed as permanent keeper of this Station by Pres. Coolidge. Went to North East for supplies. Painted in lantern. Cleaned lens to-day." Fannie's fame grew, when in 1932, she became the only—and last, female lightkeeper in the United States, earning the admiring distinction as Maryland's "Lady of the Lamp."

Despite her fame, Mrs. Salter enjoyed the quiet solitude found at Turkey Point Light Station, which was tucked away a good distance from North East on a magnificent 100-foot bluff overlooking the Elk River and Chesapeake Bay. Though many would think that Fannie's life was ideal, the opposite was true. She endured much in the way of hardship with raising her family and tending the light, not to mention the personal sacrifice of forgoing nearly all the modern conveniences society was busy clamoring to obtain.

Photo courtesy of the U.S. Coast Guard

The light and keeper's cottage, before the building was demolished

Lighthouse author Elinor DeWire noted in her book, entitled *Lighthouses of the Mid-Atlantic,* that the station at Turkey Point "was one of the last in the nation to be electrified. Its aging last keeper, Fannie Salter, lit both the lantern and her house with oil lamps from 1924 to 1944 while many of her compatriots enjoyed modern conveniences." DeWire went on to note, "the station's isolation and Salter's reclusive nature probably contributed to the slow updating of equipment."

While other lightkeepers across the country merely had to flip a switch to light their lantern during a time when electricity was becoming more commonplace in the 1930s and 1940s, Fannie was faithfully performing her duties in the old fashioned "wickie" way. Carrying lamp oil up the 35-foot tower and checking on the light at least four times daily, there was nary a time to rest for Mrs. Salter.

Her backbreaking duties became even more daunting during periods of stormy or thick weather as she was expected to wind up the striking mechanism that dropped against the station's 2,000-pound fog bell once every 10 seconds in order to warn ships of their location and potential dangers. On more than one occasion, the fog bell mechanism broke, forcing Mrs. Salter to manually strike the emergency bell by hand for extended periods of time at the exact characteristic of 10-second intervals. This had to be done regardless of the weather and length of poor visibility.

Living far away from the nearest town forced Mrs. Salter to be self-sustaining in all matters, which included many of her family's provisions. She maintained a cow at the light station, as well as turkeys, pigs, sheep and a couple of horses. Though Fannie's one daughter Olga and her husband James Crouch would live at the lighthouse for some years and provide her with a much-appreciated hand in the duties of the station, along with Mrs. Salter's son Bradley, life was challenging at every turn.

In their book *Women Who Kept the Lights,* authors Mary Louise and J. Candace Clifford note that "snow-blocked roads often marooned Mrs. Salter many weeks at a time during the winter, leaving radio and telephone as her only means of communication with the outside world." But even the telephone was hardly a reliable means of communication given the station's remoteness, as the winter ice season would often disrupt service.

An article entitled "Lady Lighthouse Keeper is Champ with

Dustmop" by Eleanor Griesemer, which appeared in the *Times Recorder*, Zanesville, Ohio, on February 26, 1947, touched on many facets of Mrs. Salter's life at Turkey Point Light Station.

At one point, the reporter captures her lightkeeping duties, noting, "Mrs. Salter's daily routine requires her to rise half an hour after sunup and extinguish the lamp, to make weather reports four times a day in the log, light the lamp half an hour before sunset, and to report when beacon lights on buoys in the vicinity need repair."

When Ms. Griesemer asked Fannie how she copes with the inevitable loneliness of her job, she merely replied, 'I like it quiet.' Mrs. Salter would retire later that year in 1947, bringing to conclusion one of the most fascinating moments in lighthouse history.

Turkey Point Lighthouse Facts and Figures

1833—Turkey Point Lighthouse was placed into service. The lighthouse originally showed a fixed white light with a daymark consisting of a white brick masonry tower and red lantern.

1849—The *List of Light-Houses, Beacons, and Floating Lights, of the United States* notes that Turkey Point Lighthouse contained eleven lamps with 15-inch reflectors, which showed a fixed white light. The light was visible 15 nautical miles in clear weather.

1850—A Letter from The Secretary of the Treasury dated December 20, 1850 notes that the keeper of the lighthouse was Elizabeth Lusby. According to the report made on Turkey Point Lighthouse, the "dwelling is of brick, and the walls were once painted, but the paint is now nearly worn off; and as it is a delightful situation, on high ground, Mrs. Lusby thinks that (the) government ought to paint it once more, for it would add much to the pleasantness of the scenery around it."

1856—The lighthouse received its first Fresnel lens.

1889—The *Annual Report of the Light-House Board* noted that "extensive improvements were made at this station. The dwelling was raised one story, by which four habitable rooms were secured, and a new front porch was built."

1895—The *Annual Report of the Light-House Board* noted that "the stable, wood shed, and smokehouse were rebuilt and some 900 running feet of fencing were renewed."

1897—The *Annual Report of the Light-House Board* noted that "the back building used as a kitchen was taken down and a new one with a porch and a pantry erected in its place. A new brick pavement was laid, two old brick pavements were relaid, and 240 feet of 3-inch plank walk was constructed."

1930—The *U.S. Coast Pilot* notes that, "Turkey Point, on the west side, at the entrance to Elk River, is a sparsely wooded bluff with abrupt slopes on the south end. The most prominent mark is Turkey Point Lighthouse, a white tower on the highest part of the bluff. Elk River, emptying into the head of Chesapeake Bay from northeastward, 16 miles above Pooles Island, is important as the approach to the western end of the Chesapeake & Delaware Canal."

1934—The *United States Lighthouse Service Light List* notes that the lighthouse was equipped with a fourth order Fresnel lens illuminated by incandescent oil vapor and also possessed a fog bell that sounded one stroke every 15 seconds.

1947—Turkey Point Lighthouse was automated.

1950—The *United States Coast Guard Light List* notes the lighthouse was equipped with a 200mm lens powered by electric.

1961—The *United States Coast Guard Light List* notes that the lighthouse showed a flashing white light every 10 seconds and from a focal plane of 129 that was visible 13 nautical miles. The light was also equipped with a red sector that was visible 8 nautical miles. The light's candlepower was 700 for the white light and 150 for the sector showing red, which covered the entrance to the Susquehanna River. The publication goes on to note that the lighthouse was "on (a) point separating Elk and Northeast Rivers," and noted that foliage partly hides the white tower.

1971—The Maryland State Forest and Park Service tore down the former keeper's dwelling, following the structure suffering from many years of vandalism and neglect.

2006—The *United States Coast Guard Light List* notes that the lighthouse shows a flashing white light every 6 seconds from a focal plane of 129 feet. Turkey Point Lighthouse is now listed as a private aid to navigation.

To learn more about the history of Turkey Point Light Station and the nonprofit organization caring for the site, contact:

Turkey Point Light Station, Inc.
P.O. Box 412
Northeast, MD 21901
(410) 287-8170
Email: info@tpls.org

Photo by Bob Trapani, Jr.

The present day Turkey Point Lighthouse, without the keeper's home and out buildings

Photo courtesy of the U.S. Coast Guard

Wolf Trap Lighthouse
Virginia

Bob Trapani, Jr.

Prayers to Escape Ice of the Great Freeze

The winter of 1893 was so harsh that the people of the day wondered if history had ever recorded a more trying time, especially when it came to the waters of the Chesapeake Bay. In fact, the public alarm caused during the extended Arctic freeze led a prominent professor by the name of John Smock, the state geologist of New Jersey, to delve deep into meteorological history records to obtain a sense of comparison.

The February 14, 1893, edition of the *Gettysburg Compiler*, noted, "From the facts and figures that he (Professor Smock) has at his command, the people who became frightened a few weeks ago when the mercury dallied around the zero point were unjustly so, and should be consoled with the information that the folks of this day and generation are not in it with the good old sires of colonial and revolutionary days for cold winters."

The calming intent of Professor Smock's report may have helped quell public fears of enduring an apocalypse-type winter, but for assistant keeper John William Thomas of the Wolf Trap Light Station, the report would prove no comfort after his world was carried away by the worst of "Old Man Winter."

The keeper's escalating fear of being surrounded by unprecedented fields of killer ice haunted him for weeks in January 1893. Author Pat Vojtech recounts in her book, *Lighting the Bay: Tales of Chesapeake Lighthouses*, the frigid scene enveloping keeper Thomas, stating, "The rivers of the Chesapeake had already been frozen solid for three weeks when on January 17, 1893, the thermometer dipped to a record-setting seventeen degrees below zero. The great freeze of the nineteenth century had settled in."

Thomas's anxieties, stemming from the long period of bone-chilling temperatures and the rising threat of the 1870 cottage screwpile lighthouse being thrown down or carried away by the ever-enlarging icebergs, mounted with each passing day.

Vojtech notes the trigger for the greatest dangers on Chesapeake Bay at this time, saying, "During the great freeze, a brief thaw created a complete breakup of the ice. Chunks of ice and snow began to move. Pushed by the wind, the ice rode up on top of other chunks and piled together into huge icebergs, as high as twenty-five to fifty feet. The lighthouses and their keepers were in danger as they had never been before."

Both official U.S. Lighthouse Service and newspaper accounts of the time fail to explain why keeper John William Thomas was alone on Wolf Trap Light during this harrowing episode, but one thing was for sure—no one was able to come to his aid since the entire Chesapeake Bay was imprisoned by the frozen hand of winter. The lighthouse was located only three miles from the bay's western shore. But for Wolf Trap keeper Thomas, this might as well have been a thousand miles away, given the impassable conditions.

In spite of the inescapable tension and isolation, keeper Thomas had to make sure the light's fourth order Fresnel lens shined its fixed white light out over the frozen seascape each night—even though the ice fields had prevented most ships and local watermen from plying the nearby waters. Imagine having to cope with the mental anguish stemming from worry that your house could be carried away at any moment, as well as enduring the unnerving vibrations caused by the massive ice floes crashing into the lighthouse. In addition, keeper Thomas had to make sure the shock of the ice against the structure's pilings did not topple the classical lens from its pedestal and subsequently catch the wooden structure on fire.

The *Daily Advocate* from Ohio recounted keeper Thomas's harrowing time in their March 4, 1893, news edition, stating, "It is not easy to appreciate the dreadful forebodings which filled his mind as day after day he watched the thickening ice, conscious as he was of the great peril which environed him, his distress signals unnoticed, with that vast field of ice expanding its mighty power against the piles and gathering additional strength every moment as it overlapped and piled up against the doomed structure."

Assessing his seemingly hopeless plight, keeper John William Thomas could think of only one thing left to do—pray!

The *Daily Advocate* went on to say, "To pray in such a crisis was a most natural thing to do, and pray he did, long and fervently, and he feels assured that his prayers were answered, for it was not very long before he descried in the distance the smoke of a steamer battling with the ice." With no knowledge of the keeper's dire situation, the steamer simply attempted to work its way up the Chesapeake Bay, but as could be expected, the transit was anything but easy.

The steamer's intense battle with the thick ice was very slow until the vessel came to a grinding halt abreast of the Wolf Trap Lighthouse. The captain brought his engines down to reassess his path through the frozen mass. In the meantime, the steamer's movements were not lost on keeper Thomas. When he realized that his prayers were answered in the form of the steamer, he decided to that he would no longer test the hand of fate.

Lightkeepers were expected to stand by their post no matter the danger, but when death's shadow loomed large as it did at this time for keeper Thomas, no one could fault him for abandoning the lighthouse to save his life.

The *Daily Advocate* conveys what happened next, noting that, "Although the steamer was some half-mile out toward the ship channel, the nervy keeper determined to abandon the station to its impending fate and make the effort to reach her. Getting upon the untried ice he proceeded toward her, waving his hat to attract the attention of those on

Photo courtesy of the U.S. Coast Guard

board." The newspaper went on to report, "When within hailing distance, he cried out lustily to the officer in command and was told to come aboard, which he did in safety. On leaving the steamer higher up in the bay for the shore he broke through the ice in eight feet of water and came near being drowned."

Shortly after the keeper's departure, the end finally came for Wolf Trap Lighthouse. On January 22, 1893, the "pancaked" icebergs proved too much for the over-strained pilings, which supported the cottage. The sheered pilings caused the lighthouse to plunge atop the ice-encrusted bay. Trapped within the jagged mass of frozen confusion, the lighthouse was held "prisoner" within the icy grip of the massive floes that were being lured down the bay to the open ocean waters on the shoulders of the tide.

Throughout the last days of Wolf Trap Light's valiant stand against the ice, the family of keeper Thomas was fraught with worry for their loved one. Years later, Mrs. Luther George would recount the fears of her siblings and her for their father's fate in a 1955 story printed in the *Virginian-Pilot* and the *Portsmouth Star.*

Mrs. George stated, "On the night of the storm, my brothers climbed up in a very tall cherry tree in our yard to look for the light. All across the Bay was only blackness. We knew the lighthouse must have been carried away. We were afraid Papa must have been lost, too."

The family had to wait a week to happily learn that keeper Thomas was rescued off the light—and survived a near drowning experience after falling through the ice further up the bay, but for the lighthouse itself, there was no happy ending.

Moving adrift on the Chesapeake Bay, no one knew where the lead-colored lighthouse was. Several days after it broke lose from its foundation, the cottage was spotted by the revenue cutter *Morrill*, approximately one mile northeast of Thimble Shoal and drifting outboard the bay's entrance at the capes.

According to author Pat Vojtech, "Only its lantern was above water, posing a real danger to navigation." The nearly submerged lighthouse needed to be removed from the open waters before it caused an accident by colliding with an unsuspecting vessel. The captain of the *Morrill* instructed his crew to put a line on the wayward beacon, which he then took in tow across the bay to the south shore. No longer a hazard to the shipping channel, and having salvaged everything of importance inside the flooded structure—including the Fresnel lens, the *Morrill* cut the lines and let the derelict lighthouse drift ashore where it met an unknown end.

Wolf Trap Lighthouse Facts & Figures

1691—According to an article in the April 1951 issue of the *Chesapeake Skipper*, Wolf Trap Shoal derives its name from a 350-ton vessel called *Their Majesties Hyred Ship Wolfe*, which was captained by George Purvis and grounded in 1691.

1821—The federal government first established a lightship to mark Wolf Trap Shoal in 1821

1861—The Wolf Trap Lightship was destroyed in 1861 during the Civil War. At the time, the Lighthouse Board noted that, "All the light-vessels from Cape Henry southward...and those in Chesapeake Bay (except Hooper's Strait and Jane's Island), have been removed and sunk or destroyed by the insurgents."

1864—A lightship was reestablished on the shoal in 1864, and remained in service for the next six years, until a lighthouse was constructed to take its place.

1870—The original Wolf Trap Lighthouse was completed and first lit on October 1. The Notice to Mariners described the beacon as "a fixed white light of the fourth order, varied by a white flash every 30 seconds." The light's focal plane was 38 feet above sea level and its beam could be seen 11 nautical miles. The structure itself was a screwpile lighthouse erected in 12 feet of water on a shoal described by the *United States Coast Pilot, 33rd Edition*, as an "area of broken ground 6 miles northward of New Point Comfort," and between the mouths of the Rappahannock and York Rivers, in Chesapeake Bay. The lighthouse was equipped with a fog bell rung by machinery at 10-second intervals.

1879—The August 21, 1879, *Daily Constitution* from Atlanta, Georgia, reported that the "*Schooner J. C. Henry*, of Philadelphia, foundered off the mouth of the Great Wicomico River, and the captain and his wife were lost. The British brig *Northern Star* and the Norwegian brig *Nordenskjold*, hence for Bayonne, have returned completely dismantled, the former having lost one man overboard, and wrecked fore and aft. A schooner has drifted in near Wolf Trap with the body of a woman lashed in the rigging."

1893—The screwpile lighthouse was destroyed by ice floes on January 22.

1894—The present Wolf Trap Lighthouse was completed and lit for the first time on September 20. The structure's caisson design stands in 16 feet of water near the outer end of the shoal area and five miles due west of a point in the main channel, 28.8 miles above the capes. The lighthouse remains an active aid to navigation and shows a flashing white light every 15 seconds from a focal plane of 52 feet. The light is visible 14 nautical miles.

1904—The October 22, 1904, *Washington Post* reported that, "The wrecking steamer *Rescue* left here this afternoon to go to the assistance of the five-masted schooner *Dorothy Palmer* reported by incoming steamers today as ashore at Wolf Trap Light in Chesapeake Bay. The *Palmer* was bound from Baltimore to Norfolk with a cargo of bituminous coal and is supposed to be resting on a huge boulder."

1909—The August 9, 1909, the *Washington Post* reported: "Sinks at Ship's Wheel...Captain Refuses to Leave Schooner When it Founders in Gale".... "News was received here today of the sinking of the of the schooner *Cary Ann Bell*, Capt. Wright, during a storm off Gwynns Island several days ago. The wrecked crew tell a tale of the captain's love for his ship—Wright deliberately going down with his hands on the wheel. At the time of the storm it was known that a schooner had been lost but the name of the vessel could not be learned. Two of the crew—both colored, arrived today and gave the details of the loss of the vessel. With a cargo of coal the schooner sailed from Havre De Grace for Hampton Roads. While off the mouth of the Rappahannock a fierce gale swept the schooner, filling it with water. According to the seamen, they begged that the captain leave the ship but he refused to do so. Taking the yawl they went adrift and were rescued by the keeper of the Wolf Trap Lighthouse and his assistants."

1918—*Lighthouse Service Bulletin*, "On November 4 John E. Morgan, second assistant keeper of Wolf Trap Light Station, Va., went to the assistance of a disabled aeroplane in the vicinity of the light station, took the occupants ashore, and beached the aeroplane, and the next day assisted in the removing of the plane to a wharf."

1919—*Lighthouse Service Bulletin*, "Assistance Rendered by Keepers"..."James B. Hurst, keeper, and V. J. Montague, assistant keeper, Wolf Trap Light Station, Va., have been commended by the Department for the assistance rendered by them in safely landing at the light station, during a severe gale, on August 27, 1919, a man, a woman, and four children, who arrived at the station, landing in a motor boat after the sinking of the schooner *Sidonia Curley* about 4 miles distant. In endeavoring to land the occupants of the boat on the east landing of the station, the keeper was twice washed from the steps, but each time managed to retain a hold on the steps with one hand. He then got the boat to the leeward of the station, with the assistance of the assistant keeper, took the occupants out, one at a time, by means of a line, the smallest child, 2 years old, being hoisted up in a bag. The party was also furnished lodging at the station for the night."

1950—The April 12, 1950, *Frederick News*, Md., reported that, "The body of one of the three crewmen missing after the tug boat *Lorraine* sank in the storm-churned waters of Chesapeake Bay early Sunday arrived here early today aboard an 83-foot Coast Guard cutter. Identified as that of Robert Mason Franklin Kellum, of Baltimore, Md., second engineer on the *Lorraine*, the body was located about 8 p.m. yesterday by the lighthouse keeper at Wolf Trap Light. Still unaccounted for are John G. Wood of Collingswood, N. J., and W. F. Jefferson, of Richmond, Va., first engineer. The sole survivor, Capt. O. P. Brown, of Norfolk, is recovering at the Marine Hospital here. Bodies of three other crewmen previously recovered and identified were those of Oliver James Hudgins, of Newport News, Va., deckhand; Norman Glen Fisher, of Lewes, Del., deckhand; and Lester Lee, of Baltimore, cook."

Photo courtesy of the U.S. Coast Guard

York Spit Lighthouse
Virginia

Bob Trapani, Jr.

Five Mariners Drown on the Doorstep of Safety

In the days of sail, ships seeking Virginia's York River leading to the historic towns of Yorktown and West Point were forced to contend with the sandy reaches of York Spit, a treacherous shoal that extends outward along the southeast side of the approach to York River.

In order to pass safely, mariners were advised to maintain a course well to the outer portion of the spit where good water at depths of 10 to 20 feet could be found. To pass on the inner side of the spit where only 1 to 6 feet of water concealed the sandy clutches of York Spit meant certain danger of grounding.

In 1855, the United States Lighthouse Service first utilized a lightship to mark this menacing underwater hazard, but by 1870, it was decided that a lighthouse would be more economical to maintain on the site. York Spit Lighthouse was thus established in 12 feet of water on the outer end of the spit, and consisted of a wooden cottage perched atop a screw-pile foundation, similar to many other Chesapeake lights. The presence of the lighthouse on the north side of the river's entrance proved invaluable as a navigational guardian but like all beacons, it was powerless to prevent every waterborne accident.

Normally, vessels passed York Spit Lighthouse with plenty of clearance, but on March 16, 1890, a schooner was not so fortunate. The sailing vessel was pushed against its will onto the sandy shoal by a terrific wind where it came to a sudden halt near the spit's northwest buoy that was tasked with preventing just such a mishap. The ship, which was now fully exposed to the ravages of wind and sea, was pounded mightily in the face of the gale. Deciding it was too dangerous to remain aboard the ill-fated schooner, the captain gave the order to abandon ship. Without a moment to lose, the captain and his four crewmen lowered the schooner's yawl boat and scurried into their only means of escape. With the York Spit Lighthouse in sight, the mariners pulled with all their might to reach safe refuge.

The boat's crew battled against the furious wind that whipped the Chesapeake Bay into a seething froth of white caps. One minute the small boat would rise wildly atop a swell before descending the gray trough in a frightening fashion. With the seas punishing the small wooden vessel and the wind refusing to be tamed, the crew could do little to control the boat as it approached the lighthouse.

The March 17, 1890, edition of Maryland's *Frederick News* ran headlines in the paper describing what happened next, stating, "Five Men Drowned—A Yawlboat Dashed against York Spit Lighthouse." Despite the horrifying notion, the headline alone could not convey the sheer terror experienced by the crew of the yawl just before they were swept under the agitated seas down to Davey Jones' Locker.

Image courtesy of Library of Congress

Drawing of a fourth order Fresnel lens in a lantern room. This lens is similar to one that would have been used in York Spit Lighthouse.

As the five mariners were fighting for their life in route to the lighthouse, a nearby steamer by the name of *Defiance*, under command of Captain Burgess, watched the tragic scene unfold. The steamer was powerless to help the crew and could only hope and pray against the sea's heavy odds that the men would reach York Spit Light safely. The gale proved too strong though, for as the yawl—which was nearly impossible to direct in the face of the howling wind—made its approach to the lighthouse, it was dashed against the light's iron screw-piles and swamped.

The captain and his crewmen were thrown overboard into the storm-tossed bay and a desperate battle for life immediately ensued. As the crew frantically clutched the iron piles of the light's foundation, their cries for help were brought to attention of the lighthouse keeper on duty. James B. Hurst, assistant keeper at York River Lighthouse, lifted the wooden hatchway leading from the structure's main gallery to the screw-pile foundation below and saw the yawl's crew struggling mightily to stay alive.

Despite the dangerous seas, keeper Hurst wasted no time lowering the light station's small boat with which he hoped to rescue the mariners. As the boat hit the water, the skipper on the nearby *Defiance* watched as the keeper descended a pile and jumped into the boat, which was bouncing like a cork. Unfortunately, no sooner did keeper Hurst pull away from the lighthouse to make his approach to the other side where the mariners were located, than the boat drifted powerlessly away from the beacon.

The sight of the keeper being carried away in the last moments of the crew's lives must have been the last straw for the men. With their strength spent in the face of the gale, their fate would be met seconds later.

The *Frederick News* noted. "The sea dashed over them with such fury that they were soon benumbed and overpowered, fell off and were drowned."

In the meantime, Captain Burgess of the *Defiance* espied keeper Hurst's boat drifting helplessly and ran along side to rescue him, which was accomplished by throwing the keeper a line and hauling him in.

According to the *Frederick News*, keeper Hurst "stated that all five of the shipwrecked men were drowned in his presence, and he was unable to render any assistance whatever on account of the violent seas dashing over everything." The news account went on to state, "it is supposed the schooner is an oyster vessel, and was trying to run into East River, but it is impossible to learn her name or the names of the drowned men. Captain Burgess of the *Defiance*, reported the disaster to the collector of customs today, who forwarded it to the lighthouse department."

York Spit Lighthouse Facts & Figures

1855—Prior to a lighthouse being built at York Spit, the United States elected to first establish a lightship to mark the navigational hazard presented by the shoal.

1861—Confederate forces removed the lightship from service during the Civil War

1867—The lightship was reestablished and remained on station until the lighthouse was completed in 1870.

1874—The *Annual Report of the Light-House Board* noted, "The lens at this station is of the fifth order, fixed red. The shoal on which the structure stands is some distance, however, from the main channel, and the light is not strong enough for the purpose required. It is proposed to substitute a lens of the fourth order, with the double-wick lamp."

1905—Keeper Filmore Hudgins and assistant Clarence W. Salter witnessed a bugeye capsize in rough seas near the lighthouse and went to the aid of the sailors in the station's dory. The lightkeepers were successful in rescuing the sailing vessel's two-man crew—Captain Arthur Hudgins and Wilbur Diggs. The two men spent the night in the lighthouse where they were provided warm clothing and food before returning to the mainland the next day.

1916—The *Lighthouse Service Bulletin* noted that "On the night of August 22 John F. Hudgins, keeper of York Spit Light Station, Va., rescued nine persons (two men, three women and four children) from a disabled launch and brought them to the light station, where they were furnished food and kept overnight."

1923—The *Lighthouse Service Bulletin* noted "On January 3, G. C. Hunley, assistant keeper of York Spit Light Station, Va., rendered assistance to the U.S. seaplane No. 5060, with two men aboard, which had become disabled in the vicinity of the light station."

1933—The *Lighthouse Service Bulletin* noted, "The following report has been received from W. J. Diggs, keeper of York Spit

Light Station, Va., on the west side of Chesapeake Bay: 'I am writing to state condition of station after storm at 6:30 a.m. (Aug. 24). Floors began to burst up, wind increasing, tide coming up. Sea higher at 8:30 a.m. Sailboat broke away. Sea breaking over deck. All lower works badly damaged. At 9:30 a.m., total wreck on lower floor. Oil tanks broke away and did a lot of damage to ironwork and sills before getting clear. Cookstove completely gone. All cooking utensils gone. Lot of decking and handrail broke away. Station is now in very bad condition. I did not think it would stand. It could not if wind had continued east, because sea was so high and coming so forceful it almost lifted house off structure a good many times.' York Spit Lighthouse is a wooden dwelling on iron piles, standing in 12 feet of water on the north side of the entrance to the York River. It has been necessary to establish a temporary light pending repairs. One keeper was ashore. The finding of the station boat on the shore unoccupied led to erroneous reports that the other keeper had been lost; he was taken off the station by fishermen."

1936—The *United States Lighthouse Service Light List* recorded that York Spit Lighthouse showed a group flashing (three flashes) red light every 10 seconds. The light also displayed two white sectors in its lantern. The lighthouse was located in 12 feet of water, on the north side of the entrance to York River. Its light showed 37 feet above high water and could be seen 11 nautical miles. The light station was also equipped with a diaphone air fog signal.

1960—The U.S. Coast Guard dismantled the historic lighthouse and replaced it with a modern light tower situated atop the original screw-pile foundation of the former lighthouse.

1997—The *Coast Pilot* notes that York Spit Light stands "30 feet above the water, is shown from a pile with a red and white diamond-shaped daymark, in depths of 12 feet near the outer end of the spit. The light is 19.8 miles above Cape Charles."

Preservation Efforts on the Chesapeake Bay

As much as the human-interest stories of the lightkeepers and their families serve as the heart and soul of lighthouses, the thought of losing any more of the physical structures themselves is a tragedy beyond comprehension to the lighthouse heritage of the Chesapeake Bay. We've already lost too many. In fact, only 34 of the bay's historic lighthouses remain today. In over a century and a half, we have lost 46 light stations to neglect, erosion, storm, vandalism and razing for safety purposes.

Without the historic lighthouse structure, how will future generations be able to experience what it is like to "walk in the steps of the keeper?"

All the stories in the annals of American lighthouse history cannot replace people's ability to touch a beacon's wood, brick and mortar or steel. Nor can these accounts—no matter how fascinating—replace the visitor's sense of smell when it comes to the saltwater air and sweet marshes that surround the lighthouses.

Both the physical lighthouse and its stories that provide a deeper human-interest meaning are essential to preserving our lighthouse heritage. Sadly though, despite the vanishing photos and oral histories of lighthouses, saving the words and images that remain often is much easier than saving the beacons themselves.

How did we arrive at the point where lighthouses are now endangered and on the verge of disappearing?

Well, similar to all facets of life, lighthouses on the Chesapeake Bay, and throughout the country, have never stopped evolving. For many decades the technology that made for brighter lights from Fresnel lenses to stronger construction of offshore sentinels like the caisson structure was embraced and celebrated as the finest in lighthouse achievements. For a time there seemed to be no stopping the improvements to the lifesaving powers and durability of our nation's lighthouses. All the while, society was unaware that with each passing advance, the lighthouse was actually slowly and systematically being rendered obsolete.

Each time the keeper's life was made easier, the lighthouse itself, as well as the men and women who tended its light, took one more step toward being forever relegated to the pages of yesteryear. Paralleling these improvements in lighthouse technology were similar breakthroughs in shipbuilding.

Evolution from wood to steel hull vessels, and from sail to steam propulsion, had dramatic impacts on lighthouses. These vital improvements enabled ships to avoid being as vulnerable to the whims of the storm winds that once wreaked havoc with wooden sailing vessels along America's treacherous coastlines.

Finally, the days of the lighthouse being manned by keepers and their families were truly numbered when the United States Lighthouse Service began establishing automatic acetylene lights during the 1920s.

Another invention of that era, the radiobeacon, became the first electronic navigational advance that would further help doom the critical importance of lighthouses. Over the years, this was followed by radar and now, in the present day, differential Global Positioning System (GPS) satellite navigational technology. Even the lowly buoy, which can be placed in vast numbers at economical prices, and require only periodic care, played a noteworthy part in the demise of the lighthouse.

The lighthouses of the Chesapeake Bay were no exception to this irresistible lure of pushing the boundaries of man's knowledge and capabilities. In the wake of fascinating scientific advances, some lighthouses were eventually discontinued—their lifesaving powers rendered ineffective by a combination of technology and declining commerce in certain regions of the bay.

Other beacons fell victim to erosion's eternal march, oftentimes their doom accelerated by the raging elements riding the shoulders of a summertime hurricane or winter's icy gales. Even the automated lighthouses, though still utilized for navigation, suffer from various stages of deterioration, a direct correlation to the removal of the keepers and the care they provided to the structures, as well as the persistent lack of money to invest in their preservation over the past 40-plus years.

In the end, automated lights and advances in electronic navigation not only reduced the importance of lighthouses, but these factors also forever changed the role of the lightkeeper as well. Hans Christian Adamson, author of the 1955 book entitled *Keepers of the Lights*, noted, "There is a cost, a price, attached to everything. With respect to our lighthouses, lightships, and other aids the price has been the foregoing change in emphasis."

Adamson, in prophetic fashion over 51 years ago, went on to say, "It is no longer the keeper and his light. Now it is the lights and their keepers. Gone from the lighthouses are the picturesque salt-water characters with their wives and children who helped to run the lights. Their places, except for a few instances, have been taken by snappy young men who wear the Coast Guard uniform with well-deserved pride. But as times goes on, one sees the passing of even Coast Guard crews from the solitary sentries of the sea because, more and more, automatic equipment takes the place of devices that require human attention."

Thomas Point Shoal Lighthouse

Before the author left the Delmarva region for Maine in May 2005, he had the privilege of being a very small part of the latest lighthouse preservation project in the Chesapeake Bay. On May 1, 2004, the Thomas Point Shoal Lighthouse, located just off Annapolis, Maryland—and widely deemed the icon of the Chesapeake Bay—was granted new keepers of the light.

A public/private partnership consisting of the United States Lighthouse Society, its Chesapeake Chapter, Annapolis Maritime Museum, City of Annapolis and Maryland's Anne Arundel County was formed to preserve this timeless treasure under the provisions of the National Historic Lighthouse Preservation Act.

The author observed firsthand the passion, dedication and talents of the light's newest keepers—Henry Gonzalez, Jane Cox, Sandy Clunies, Tom Wade, Cullen Chambers, Anne Puppa and Jeffrey Holland—just to name a few.

These volunteers have come together, not only to ensure that Thomas Point Shoal Lighthouse will be saved, but also to share its history with the general public in memorable fashion.

Henry Gonzalez is playing a vital role in the preservation of Thomas Point Shoal Lighthouse, wearing three distinctly different lighthouse hats as the United States Lighthouse Society's (USLHS) Vice-President for East Coast Operations, President of the Chesapeake Chapter of the USLHS and Manager of the Thomas Point Shoal Lighthouse.

According to Gonzalez, "The lighthouse will be open to the public for tours all throughout our ongoing preservation activities, starting in the summer of 2006. The tours will originate at the Annapolis Maritime Museum, home of our shoreside interpretation center."

The lighthouse tours and interpretation will enable visitors to see firsthand the unique historical value of Thomas Point Shoal Lighthouse and the urgent need to ensure that the gorgeous beacon receives proper preservation and maintenance. Gonzalez states "It is very important that we act now to preserve Thomas Point Shoal Lighthouse for generations to come. Thomas Point Shoal is the last lighthouse of its kind. It is the last intact cottage-style screwpile lighthouse still located in its original offshore location."

Gonzalez goes on to say, "Where once there were more than 40 such screwpile lighthouses throughout the Chesapeake Bay, now only Thomas Point remains on guard, protecting the Bay's mariners and watermen. In recognition of its uniqueness, it was designated as a National Historic Landmark in 1999, and is only one of nine lighthouses in the country with this special honor.

"Although the lighthouse was automated and unmanned in 1986, the Coast Guard has maintained it in very good shape, so our preservation efforts are not huge. But that is also why we need to act now, while there is still time, and while she is in good shape—before she suffers the fate of other

Photo courtesy of Henry Gonzalez

Jane Cox, Henry Gonzalez and Cullen Chambers, of the Thomas Point Shoal Lighthouse project, near Sandy Point Light

Chesapeake Bay lighthouses close by, like the Sandy Point Shoal Lighthouse, which although still operational, is in a sad state of disrepair and probably beyond preserving."

Thomas Point Shoal Lighthouse is fortunate to have the very finest of keepers—and because of their commitment, one of the crown jewels of the Chesapeake Bay will be preserved for future generations to appreciate and enjoy, but this is not the only exciting lighthouse preservation project in the Bay.

Shining Examples of Other Chesapeake Lighthouse Preservation Projects

Hooper Strait Lighthouse (Md.)—Built 1879, automated 1954

The vision of the Chesapeake Bay Maritime Museum, back during a time when lighthouse preservation was not as commonplace, not only saved the Hooper Strait Lighthouse, but also set a precedent that gave hope to decaying offshore lights in the Bay. Faced with demolition in 1966, Hooper Strait Light was acquired by the museum from the U.S. Coast Guard and placed on its new land-base foundation 40 miles up the bay in St. Michaels on November 9, 1966.

Photo courtesy of Library of Congress

To learn more about the Hooper Strait Lighthouse and its caretakers at the Chesapeake Bay Maritime Museum, contact:

Chesapeake Bay Maritime Museum
213 N. Talbot St.
P.O. Box 636
St. Michaels, MD 21663
(410) 745-2916
www.cbmm.org

Drum Point Lighthouse (Md.)—Built 1883, automated 1960

The Drum Point Light stood deteriorating for 15 long years, from 1960 to 1975, as preservationists from Calvert County, Md., coped with government red tape over the transfer process and ceaseless vandalism that very nearly erased the lighthouse altogether, before it could be saved.

By March 1975 the Calvert Marine Museum in Solomons Island was successful in obtaining title to the lighthouse and hired a construction firm to move the 41-ton screwpile structure two miles up the Patuxent River to its new land-base site at the museum. Today, the Drum Point Lighthouse is fully restored and open to the general public for educational tours.

To learn more about the Drum Point Lighthouse and its caretakers at the Calvert Marine Museum, contact:

Calvert Marine Museum
P.O. Box 97
Solomons Island, MD 20688
(410) 326-2042
www.calvertmarinemuseum.com

Photo by Bob Trapani, Jr.

Piney Point Lighthouse (Md.)—Built 1836, automated 1964

Ownership of Piney Point Lighthouse was transferred from the U.S. Coast Guard to St. Mary's County and the Department of Recreation and Parks in 1980. The county appointed stewardship of the lighthouse to the St. Clement's Island Museum, which has worked hard caring for the lighthouse and developing a museum on the light station property that shares the local region's maritime heritage with thousands of visitors each year.

To learn more about the Piney Point Lighthouse, contact:

Piney Point Lighthouse Museum and Park
c/o St. Clement's Island Museum
Colton's Point, MD 20626
(301) 769-2222
www.co.saint-marys.md.us/recreate/

Photo by Bob Trapani, Jr.

Bob Trapani, Jr.

You and I
New Keepers of the Lights

Who are the modern keepers of the lights? The answer is you and I. Everyday people from all walks of life are joining together and volunteering to save America's lighthouse heritage while there is still time to help.

In the Chesapeake Bay there is one group that stands out for its love and commitment to many of the region's lighthouses when it comes to working to save lighthouses—the nonprofit Chesapeake Chapter of the United States Lighthouse Society. This tireless organization advocates for the preservation and educational utilization of all lighthouses dotting the Chesapeake Bay. The Chapter also serves as a key partner in the preservation of Thomas Point Shoal Lighthouse, arguably the icon of the entire Chesapeake Bay.

The Chesapeake Chapter thrives as keepers of the lights thanks to their dedicated volunteers. Learning why volunteerism is so important to lighthouse preservation is one thing, but hearing what it means for volunteers to "give back" to the lighthouse preservation they love in their own words is even more special.

Why not consider volunteering for your favorite lighthouse project today—and like so many others become a "keeper of the light?"

Following are some comments by people who have made that decision.

People often don't value something until it is gone, and by then, it's too late. By preserving the lighthouses in this area we are saving an important part of history and honoring those in the lighthouse service that often sacrificed so much, and in a small way, we become part of that history.

Volunteering is also a social thing. You meet so many people with varied backgrounds and they make your life so much richer for knowing them. Lighthouse folks are some of the most generous people I know. It is also a way to feel that you are making a valuable contribution to the future in a way that for many of us our "day job" doesn't provide. I've found one person can make a difference and when you get a group of people working together, you can make even a bigger difference. Volunteering is definitely something I can look on and be proud of.

—Anne Puppa

Chesapeake Chapter, United States Lighthouse Society

After many years of visiting these and other lighthouses and lightships, we decided that we wanted to help in the preservation of them so that they would be around for future generations. Helping to preserve these beautiful beacons has brought us much joy. You might say it has become a passion of ours! All of these volunteer opportunities have allowed us to give something back to our country and the various organizations that maintain these historic sites. As a bonus we also have had the opportunity to meet some great people and make some new friendships! Volunteering is great fun!

—Lauren & Paula Liebrecht

Chesapeake Chapter, United States Lighthouse Society

Photo by Bob Trapani, Jr.

Heading off to work at a lighthouse are, from left, twins Paula and Lauren Liebrecht and Anne Puppa.

Bob Trapani, Jr.

Lighthouses and lightships are part of the treasured maritime history of our country. It is no longer just the elements that ravage these icons but vandalism and neglect as well. I feel privileged to be a part of the heroic effort to preserve their architecture and history.

I was born and raised at the head of the Chesapeake Bay, just steps away from Concord Point Lighthouse. For the past 34 years, I have lived in southern Maryland surrounded by Piney Point, Point Lookout, Drum Point and Cove Point lights.

I used to sit on the point, when I first moved down here, and wonder what could be done to stop the deterioration of Cedar Point (now lost). However small my contribution is, I feel at least I am helping keep the "hounds of destruction" at bay.

—Sandra L. Sableski
Chesapeake Chapter, United States Lighthouse Society

Working on Fort Washington Light/Bell Tower, Thomas Point Shoal Light and the Assateague Life-Saving Station has given us a chance to honor the memory of past lightkeepers and share in the wonderful camaraderie of fellow preservationists. Fort Washington Light is one of only a handful of beacons still standing and active on the Potomac River. Our efforts were especially evident after last year's Maryland Lighthouse Challenge, with the new wooden siding and a fresh coat of paint, the tower sparkled with renewed radiance.

—Tony & Alma Pasek
Chesapeake Chapter, United States Lighthouse Society

Photo by Bob Trapani, Jr.

Lighthouse preservationists Alma and Tony Pasek, beside a DCB-36 aero beacon

Epilogue

'Admire Me, Cherish Me, but Please Help Save Me!'

Year after year, I tower majestically over the shorelines and waters of our great country while presenting a romantic appearance that is admired and loved by young and old alike. I symbolize the essence of strength, the virtue of steadfast dedication and proudly represent the unique heritage of my community.

I stand in lasting tribute to the dedication and great sacrifice of the keepers and their families who kept my light burning bright through many a storm and hardship. In fact, my legacy stands honorably in the halls of time for the protection I afforded mankind, as fate would permit.

Since the birth of the United States, I have sent out a guiding light to those seeking a better way of life, as well as for mariners who worked to harvest the great bounty the sea or transported precious goods—ensuring they were brought home safely to their loved ones each and every night.

Time and technology may have diminished my lifesaving powers in the 21st century, but these forces can do little to fade the glory of my service to America and her people.

I was built to serve and to last while I was needed, but unfortunately, progress seems to have little purpose for me now. As a static symbol of our nation's glorious past, I am hard pressed to keep pace with a society that displays an insatiable desire for the speed of life and electronic wizardry.

Thankfully, caring groups and individuals throughout our country have recognized my plight and stepped forward to save my kind. Yet many other of my comrades have fallen victim to the effects of erosion, neglect, and, sadly, even complacency and indifference to my plight.

I am happy that thousands of folks climb my steps to appreciate the beauty and breathtaking view my lofty perch affords. My image adorns countless homes in the form of resin models depicting my likeness to clothing that says you love me. You've taken many pictures of my stately presence for which I'm most flattered. Yet I plead with you to stop for a moment to take a closer look at my brick, mortar and steel, for all is not well.

Automation, budget cuts, vandalism and Mother Nature have combined to subtly compromise my strength. You must remember that while you seek safe refuge in the warm comforts of your home, by design I must continue to muster the strength to stand defiantly in the face of the most terrifying tempests. Even on calm days, my brick, mortar and steel suffer the slow but exacting toll from the effects of salt air, moisture and the tides.

Despite all that is against me, I will not complain. Instead, I continue to stand and serve with all my might until the last ounce of my strength has been used. But please, remember, time marches on whether you notice or not.

If you don't come to my aid now, there will come a day I will no longer be there for you. I'd like to banish the very thought of my demise but I am powerless without your helping hand. Much in the way of your time, money and unwavering passion will be required in this preservation battle of attrition.

There is no question that the course of life will test your resolve for me—but am I not worth your very best?

If you do not fail me in my greatest hour of need, you have my word I will not fail you in the coming years, as I shine a bright light on our nation's proud maritime heritage and pathway to boundless tomorrows. With your love, passion and hard work, I will continue to glow as a beacon of freedom and prosperity for future Americans. I will help teach your children what dedication, valor, sacrifice and unfailing service mean and how these qualities symbolize our great country and her fine people.

Time is not on my side though. They will not build my kind again. My light will shine on only a little while longer if you don't help me now. As your lifelong friend, won't you please answer my desperate call for help before its too late?

Sincerely,

Your Favorite Lighthouse

Selected Bibliography

Bay Beacons: Lighthouses of the Chesapeake Bay by Linda Turbyville

Lighting the Bay: Tales of Chesapeake Lighthouses by Pat Vojtech

U.S. Coast Guard Light List Volumes

U.S. Lighthouse Service Light List Volumes

U.S. Coast Pilot Volumes

Maryland Lighthouses of the Chesapeake Bay by F. Ross Holland

Forgotten Beacons: The Lost Lighthouses of the Chesapeake Bay by Patrick Hornberger & Linda Turbyville

Chesapeake Lights, the official newsletter of the United States Lighthouse Society's Chesapeake Chapter

Keeper's Log, the official journal of the United States Lighthouse Society

Keepers of the Lights, Hans Christian Adamson

Chesapeake Chapter web site: www.cheslights.org

United States Coast Guard Historian's web site: www.uscg.mil/hq/g-cp/history/collect.html

United States Lighthouse Service Annual Reports, Inspection Reports and Official Correspondence such a letters from The Secretary of the Treasury

United States Lighthouse Service Bulletins

Women Who Kept the Lights by Mary Louise Clifford and J. Candace Clifford

Havre de Grace: An Informal History edited by Peter A. Jay

Lighthouses of the Mid-Atlantic by Elinor DeWire

Phantom in the Bedchamber by Ed Okonowicz

Lighthouse Digest Magazine: www.lhdigest.com

Russ Rowlett's web site: www.unc.edu/~rowlett/lighthouse/

Cape Henry: First Landing, First United States Lighthouse by Norma Elizabeth and Bruce Roberts

Chesapeake Bay Program web site: www.chesapeakebay.net

Times Recorder, Zanesville, Ohio, February 26, 1947

Decatur Weekly Republican, Decatur, Illinois, October 29, 1891

Baltimore Sun, Baltimore, Maryland, October 12, 1891

Herald Torch & Light, Hagerstown, Maryland, November 12, 1891

Arizona Republican, Arizona, December 10, 1891

Thomas Point Shoal Lighthouse: Letters penned by various light-keepers on station, provided by Sandy Clunies, Certified Genealogist

Indiana County Gazette, Indiana, July 29, 1891

The Daily Times, Maryland, October 29, 1972

The Frederick News, Maryland, March 17, 1890; May 1948; November 27, 1948; December 15, 1948; April 12, 1950

Salisbury Times, Maryland, December 31, 1956; February 20, 1957; April 30, 1960; March 18, 1961

Washington Post, Washington, D.C., October 22, 1904; July 1907; January 28, 1908; August 9, 1909; December, 1909

Lima News, Ohio, February, 1957

Berkshire Eagle, Pittsfield, Massachusetts, February 19, 1957

Chester Times, Pennsylvania, October 24, 1877

The Baltimore News, Baltimore, Maryland, February 28, 1936

Nebraska State Journal, Nebraska, December 5, 1900

Advocate, Newark, Ohio, January 9, 1913

Athens Messenger, Ohio, December 10, 1931

The Baltimore American, Baltimore, Maryland, 1960

Iowa City Daily Press, Iowa, February 14, 1912

Sheboygan Press, Wisconsin, May 23, 1970

Gettysburg Compiler, Pennsylvania, February 14, 1893

Daily Advocate, Ohio, March 4, 1893

Daily Constitution, Atlanta, Georgia, August 21, 1879

About the Author

Bob Trapani, Jr., was born in Pottstown, Pennsylvania, and now resides in Wells, Maine, with his wife, Ann-Marie, and their three children—Nina, Katrina and Dominic.

On May 1, 2005, Bob assumed the position of executive director for the American Lighthouse Foundation, headquartered in Wells, Maine. The American Lighthouse Foundation is presently the steward of 22 historic lighthouses throughout New England and owns the Museum of Lighthouse History, also located in Wells.

Prior to this, Bob served as the president for the Delaware River & Bay Lighthouse Foundation in Lewes, Delaware, which he co-founded in 1999. During his tenure in Delaware, Bob helped the organization secure ownership of Harbor of Refuge Lighthouse from the Department of the Interior through the National Historic Lighthouse Preservation Act. Under his leadership, the Delaware River & Bay Lighthouse Foundation also obtained a long-term lease of Liston Range Rear Light from the U.S. Coast Guard and forged a ground-breaking partnership with the Delaware River & Bay Authority for the preservation of Delaware Breakwater East End Light.

In addition to his passion for lighthouse preservation, Bob served four years, from 2000 to 2003, as the executive director of the Delaware Seashore Preservation Foundation, caretakers of the historic 1876 Indian River Life-Saving Station Museum, located in Rehoboth Beach, Delaware. During his tenure at the lifesaving station, Bob authored his first book—*Journey Along the Sands: A History of the Indian River Life-Saving Station,* in 2002.

He also enjoys volunteering his time to the United States Coast Guard as an Auxiliarist, having spent five years with the USCG Aids to Navigation Team, Cape May, New Jersey (2000-2005). He now works with Coast Guard aids to navigation teams in Maine. Bob was awarded the prestigious U.S. Coast Guard Auxiliary Meritorious Service Award for his contributions to the field of aids to navigation from 2001 through 2003.

Bob also enjoys maritime writing and is a contributing writer for *Lighthouse Digest* magazine and *Wreck & Rescue,* a publication of the United States Life-Saving Service Heritage Association. Bob has penned *Lighthouses of New Jersey and Delaware: History, Mystery, Legend & Lore,* which was published by Myst and Lace Publishing Company, Elkton, Maryland, in 2005. He has also authored *Delaware Lighthouses: A Brief History,* which is due to be released in November 2006.

More titles from Myst and Lace Publishers, Inc.

Regional History

Mystery Novels

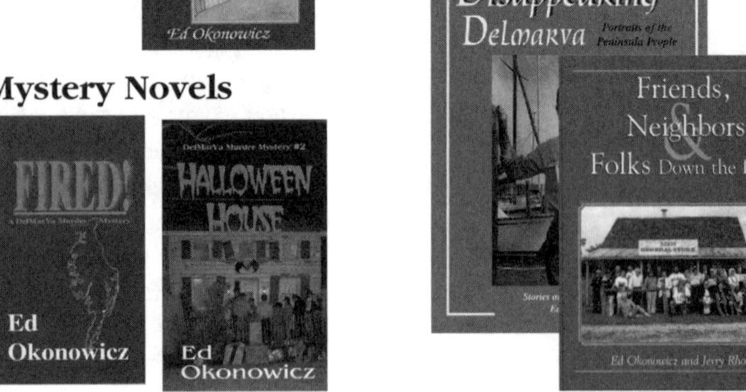

For more information about these books, which are available at some local and chain bookstores, visit the web site:**www.mystandlace.com**, send an e-mail to Ed Okonowicz at edo@mystandlace.com or call (410) 398-5013. The books also are available through www.Amazon.com

. . . and you thought sharks were the only danger at the beach!

In *Terrifying Tales of the Beaches and Bays* and the sequel, award-winning author and storyteller Ed Okonowicz shares eerie accounts of spirits roaming the shore.

128 pages
5 1/2" x 8 1/2"
softcover
ISBN 1-890690-06-6

Read about:

- A river pilot's memorable New Year's Eve cruise
- Desperate Confederates escaping from an island prison
- Serious seekers of pirate gold
- Fishermen stranded in the icy Chesapeake Bay
- Lighthouse keepers still tending a long-gone beacon
- A most unusual "catch of the day"
- Ocean City's "Trash Rat"
- and more . . . .

$9.95 each

128 pages
5 1/2" x 8 1/2"
softcover
ISBN 1-890690-10-4

Delmarva beach-reading best sellers

48 pages
5 1/2" x 8 1/2"
softcover
ISBN 1-890690-07-4

$6.95

Treasure Hunting

by Eddie Okonowicz

Dig up your own hidden treasures with this excellent "how to" book

This book is loaded with tips on using a metal detector to hunt for relics and treasure, plus photos of numerous historical finds.

Visit our web site at: www.mystandlace.com

To Order our Books

Name ____

Address____

City_________________________State_________Zip Code___________

Phone _(_____)________________e-mail:_____________________

To receive the free *Spirits Speaks* newsletter and information on future volumes, public tours and events, send us your e-mail address, visit our web site [www.mystandlace.com] or fill out the above form and mail it to us.

I would like to order the following books:

Quantity	Title	Price	Total
_______	**Lighthouses of Maryland and Virginia**	**$11.95**	_______
_______	**Lighthouses of New Jersey and Delaware**	**$11.95**	_______
_______	Civil War Ghosts at Fort Delaware	$11.95	_______
_______	Baltimore Ghosts	$11.95	_______
_______	Baltimore Ghosts Teacher's Guide	$ 8.95	_______
_______	Terrifying Tales of the Beaches and Bays	$ 9.95	_______
_______	Terrifying Tales 2 of the Beaches and Bays	$ 9.95	_______
_______	Treasure Hunting	$ 6.95	_______
_______	Pulling Back the Curtain, Vol I	$ 8.95	_______
_______	Opening the Door, Vol II (second edition)	$ 9.95	_______
_______	In the Vestibule, Vol IV	$ 9.95	_______
_______	Presence in the Parlor, Vol V	$ 9.95	_______
_______	Crying in the Kitchen, Vol VI	$ 9.95	_______
_______	Up the Back Stairway, Vol VII	$ 9.95	_______
_______	Horror in the Hallway, Vol VIII	$ 9.95	_______
_______	Phantom in the Bedchamber, Vol IX	$ 9.95	_______
_______	Possessed Possessions	$ 9.95	_______
_______	Possessed Possessions 2	$ 9.95	_______
_______	Ghosts	$ 9.95	_______
_______	Fired! A DelMarVa Murder Mystery (DMM)	$ 9.95	_______
_______	Halloween House (DMM#2)	$ 9.95	_______
_______	Disappearing Delmarva	$38.00	_______
_______	Friends, Neighbors & Folks Down the Road	$30.00	_______
_______	Stairway over the Brandywine, A Love Story	$ 5.00	_______

*Md residents add 5% sales tax.
Please include $2.00 postage for the first book, and 50 cents for each additional book.
Make checks payable to:
Myst and Lace Publishers

Subtotal___________
Tax*______________
Shipping _________
Total _____________

All books are signed by the author. If you would like the book(s) personalized, please specify to whom.

Mail to: Ed Okonowicz
1386 Fair Hill Lane
Elkton, Maryland 21921

Visit our web site at: www.mystandlace.com